The Youthlink Story

FELIX DONNELLY

Allen & Unwin/Port Nicholson Press

First published in 1987
by Allen & Unwin New Zealand Limited,
in association with the Port Nicholson Press,
60 Cambridge Terrace, Wellington,
New Zealand

Allen & Unwin Australia Pty Ltd,
NCR House, 8 Napier Street, North Sydney,
NSW 2060, Australia

Allen & Unwin (Publishers) Ltd,
40 Museum Street, London WC1, England

Allen & Unwin Inc.,
50 Cross Street, Winchester, Mass. 01890, USA

ISBN 0 86861 778 4
All royalties from the sale of this book
will go towards the work of caring for young people in need.

Cover photograph by Ken Browning
Design: Missen & Geard
Typeset by Graphicraft Ltd, Hong Kong
Printed by Colorcraft Ltd, Hong Kong

In appreciation of so many young people and adults who have shared in a dream that has brought measures of pain, joy and growth, and that has been a statement of faith in the capacity for love and development within us all.

Contents

Introduction
A Vision

I sat in total darkness, cooped up in a space that allowed sitting room only. On either side were small grilles covered with mesh and sealed off by sliding panels of wood: the traditional Catholic confessional. Sliding the right-hand panel across, and not looking at the outline of a face on the other side, I heard the usual 'Bless me Father, for I have sinned.' The voice was young and nervous. I guessed it was that of a fifteen-year-old male. The sins were listed — lies, disobedience and then a pause, as though more was to come. 'Are you finding it difficult to tell me any more?' No reply, and then the sobs.

More than ever before I resented the barrier that existed between myself and the person seeking help. He could be invited to meet me privately afterwards, but from experience I knew that would not happen. Struggling with the impossible communication barrier of a grille, I tried to comfort the youth. It emerged that he was in a vulnerable situation, and being destroyed by it. His mother's de facto husband was alternatively beating him for misbehaviour or sexually interfering with him. His mother appeared unwilling to do anything.

The youth had tried running away, but that had resulted in more violence and tension. I suggested ways of dealing with his stress. He appeared to listen. He asked was there anywhere he could run away to, where he would be safe and not have to meet with his stepfather or mother. I told him of the possibility of arranging a private home for him or contacting a government welfare agency. He did not want that. Eventually he said he must go. With as much caring as I could express, I invited him to meet with me in privacy to see what could be done to help further. He thanked me. As I gave absolution, I realised how strongly I felt about my dream of a home to care for at risk and needy youth.

After the boy had left the confessional, I sat in a state of distress, wishing I could have offered more to the youth. Later in the presbytery I tried to share my desire to set up a caring, safe base for youth with the elderly parish priest. He dismissed what I was saying before I had time to explain. 'Encouraging the break-up of families' and 'what the young needed was firm discipline' were the insensitive responses laid on me. I was to hear them for most of the years to come from many people, whom I sought assistance from in making a dream become real.

I'm not entirely clear about when the vision first began and why it grew in intensity with the passing years. I do know that it goes back to my own adolescence and certainly had much to do with my becoming a priest. Analysts delight in finding explanations for altruistic behaviour, or in exposing the motivation of anyone who wants to work with the needy and oppressed. Often it is made to sound like an inadequacy in the helper, or a fulfilment of personal frustrations. To some extent those factors are present in most human endeavours; but they do not totally explain what drives people to make personal sacrifices, and often suffer severe disappointments and rejections, to assist those in need.

I admit to being a sensitive person, often feeling others' pain. At school I was very aware of those commonly put down as 'the lame ducks', and the shattering experiences they had to endure from callous children. In those days terms such as 'self-esteem' or 'self-concept' were not used, but knocking one's confidence and instilling a sense of inferiority were most actively promoted. I had a vague ambition to do something in my life to help others; it was focused by the film 'Boys' Town', starring Spencer Tracy and Mickey Rooney. The story of Father Flanagan's home for runaway youth excited my young mind and he became my hero.

Years later, when I went to great lengths during a visit to the United States of America to stop off in Nebraska to visit his original Boys' Town, I was disappointed. The concept had changed and the place no longer took in the type of youth who had been Father Flanagan's concern. It seemed to have become a place for respectable youth with some family problems — a well-run institution looking more like a boarding school than the home depicted on the screen and fostered in my imagination. No delinquent youth were in evidence.

Seven years' spartan existence in a Catholic house which trained young men for the priesthood provided hours of time for daydreaming about my future work. Some form of home for the needy young always figured prominently. I made a special study of education during that period, seeing it as an important area in my future work. When I left the seminary and worked in Waihi parish, I took up extramural university studies, again focusing on education as my main area of interest.

The work I did in Waihi with young people heightened my desire to provide a stable environment for those who were deprived of secure family life, or who needed an experience of group living in order to move easily into maturity. While there, I tried to get support from Bishop Delargey to buy an acre of land at Waihi Beach, in order to establish a live-in setting for young people. The land was cheap, but the Bishop cautioned against the proposal.

When I was transferred to Auckland to complete my university studies and to take on an administrative post with the Catholic Education Office, I looked out for an opportunity to combine school inspection visits in the upper North Island with the establishment of a residential home for youth in trouble. I realised toward the end of my university studies that in terms of getting into social work within the Church's framework, I had made a mistake in taking an education degree. It became clear, too late, that I should have done a psychology or sociology course. The fact that I was appointed to educational work in the diocese of Auckland meant that my fate was settled.

Compromise appeared the only way to satisfy my desire to work with socially needy youth. I was working toward a Fulbright Scholarship to Harvard University to take a degree in sociology when an opportunity arose to run a Church-based home in Curran Street, Ponsonby, for delinquent teenage boys. I jumped at the chance of working in a personal way with youth as opposed to the formal relationship of a school examiner, where for the first time I had found the young responding to me with attitudes ranging from distrust to fear.

My work with the Curran Street Hostel (Bosco House) only lasted a year, as I was sent by Church authorities to study religious education at a European university. During the year I had made mistakes: thinking I could be an Inspector of Catholic Schools, primary and secondary, complete my Masters in Education, and write new syllabi for religious education in schools, as well as oversee a twenty-three-bed hostel. But I loved the experience of living with the young people and trying to develop programmes that would help them to fit into life. The major thing I learnt was how difficult it was to run a home of that kind and be answerable for youthful misbehaviour to Church authorities.

I was constantly aware of a shadow overhanging what went on, with accountability being seen in terms of the 'good name of the Church'. Nude posters of women were ripped off the boys' bedroom walls, alcohol and females were both forbidden in the home, and success was measured on a scale of non-offending. Recidivism was judged a failure, and breaking rules was grounds for dismissal. I lived with considerable nervous tension, trying to please all my masters as well as provide a home for the residents.

3

When I was sent to Belgium, I tried to support the home from a distance, but within a few months learnt that it had been closed down: a resident had threatened with a knife the priest looking after the Hostel. I was determined to re-establish Bosco House as soon as I completed my studies in Europe. Naively, I believed the authorities would allow this. Obsessed with that intention, I turned down opportunities of work in Brussels and study in Washington.

On my return to New Zealand, I tried all my persuasive powers to get the Archbishop to allow me to reopen the Curran Street property. Neither my efforts nor those of the late Mr Justice Sinclair, who made his own approach to the elderly prelate, were of any value. I was told that all my energies were to be directed toward education. I was disconsolate.

A supportive group of Catholic men, who knew how much I wanted to get a project going, offered backing, and we had some preliminary meetings. They were Jim Anderton, now a Labour Member of Parliament, Mr Maurice Casey, now a well-known High Court Judge, Ian Shirley, now Professor of Social Work Training at Massey University, and John Graham, who has been the voluntary accountant for our whole operation ever since its inception. While awaiting an opportunity to set up a home, I supported some needy young people in a private way in a large house in Owens Road, Epsom. This helped to lessen the stress I was under in not being able to carry out my most pressing wish.

During this period I was able to shape my vision more realistically. I came a step closer to its achievement when, in 1969, I helped establish the Youthline Phone Counselling Service in Auckland. It became clear very soon after the young people began answering the phones that there was a need for some of the callers to have a change of environment, as well as any counselling the agency could provide. This provided a spur to getting a home established.

My chance came in 1971, when I was appointed to the Auckland Medical School as a lecturer in the Department of Community Health. The Bishop tried to get accommodation for me in a Marist Brothers' training establishment, but fortunately that did not happen. I quickly came up with my own alternative, a house in Lloyd Avenue, Mt Albert, that John Graham and I had discovered. We bought it for $18,000, without any capital, but with a great deal of faith.

The vision I had then is still clear. It flooded into my mind the Friday night when I first moved into Lloyd Avenue House. I stood on the upstairs verandah and looked out over much of Mt

Albert and beyond, to Mt Eden and the distant city. This would be a home that was unique. It would provide a haven for young people who needed a sanctuary, or security, or a chance to change their life-styles. It would be open to females as well as males and would operate under one rule only — that we would care about each other. For eight years it was able to be run under that maxim.

Some eight years later I was to write in *Candles in the Wind*:

I have an impossible dream. To establish a communal living situation in which all those living together really care about one another. After eight years of trying I have not given up. I know that what I hope for will never be fully realised, but even the trying for such a Utopia is well worth the effort. My initial concept was to get needy youth together and work with them to establish a group that would be a healing experience for all the deprivations they had suffered, and that it would generate a warmth that would help them blossom.

I believed in my vision that treating people with respect, especially when they were young, must sink deep within them, and at some point would be a healing factor in their lives. I believed (and still do) that most of us only attain a fraction of our potential to be real, through a lack of warm, empathic and accepting living, in which we are loved unconditionally and allowed to be ourselves. What I thought about included the hope that parents would be given a chance to improve fractured relationships with their children and to become closer to them through the time of separated living. My vision highlighted a warm and caring environment, with barriers to loving being removed and young people being encouraged to change because they were loved and because they found themselves recognised and affirmed for what they were, rather than what they might become. In my vision, my own example and sensitivity to them was paramount.

The living out of that vision over the past fifteen and more years has been the major preoccupation of my life. On reflection there have been times when I have faltered, felt exhausted and wondered about what I was achieving. But the vision has persisted even into the complexity and extent of the present operation with all its facets. What has never changed for me, and I believe for those who have shared my vision, is the vulnerability of the young, their openness to change and their responsiveness to genuine caring. I have also felt the genuine regard of so many of them, and that has given me energy to continue.

The Youthlink Story is one of thousands of young lives, of suffering and disappointments, often of human tragedy, of failures and successes, and above all of change in response to altering needs. It is in its own way a record of a changing world, the pressures on present day parents, and the insecurity increasingly common among the young. Behind the techniques and programmes outlined in these pages, the dominant thought is the personal worth of the individual, and the belief that damaged children and youth can and deserve to be allowed to grow beyond such experiences. It is not a given programme that has achieved any of the successes of Youthlink, but a basic faith in the value of the individual and their capacity, under the right circumstances, to grow.

PART ONE

The Development of Youthlink

(1)

Fifteen Years
in the Making

Starting my own venture at Lloyd Avenue, Mt Albert, was an exciting experience — taking over an old two-storey building, and beginning to form a programme to care for teenage males. At the start it was not possible to incorporate females, especially as I was single and no women were then involved in the venture. The very first night I moved in, I received a phone call from a university student whom I had been counselling. Colin was suicidal. He became the first resident of thousands who have lived in the Youthlink Homes.

At first, I did not involve the residents as much in decision-making as I was later to do. Elected representatives met with small groups of residents, and then with myself, in our living as a community. I also used some of the leaders in the Youthline Phone Counselling Service to run groups on Sunday afternoons, dealing with individual and communal living problems.

We tended to grow in multiples of seven, so over the years I was able to experiment with ideal numbers to run a home on. The programmes appeared to go much better when the numbers were larger than when they were under ten. They also improved when, after a year's existence, we slowly introduced females. A house close to the Lloyd Avenue one was rented to me for a year while its owner was overseas. Our first female residents and a couple of males moved into it, and gradually other females were placed in the larger house. Their presence changed the environment. The level of discussion improved, the coarseness of language lessened, and a greater degree of sensitivity appeared among residents toward each other. This softening improved the overall living in the Home.

At the same time as young women joined us, the numbers were increased to twenty-four. They could not all fit into the one Home, so we rented several nearby flats and houses, placing the more responsible youth in those. I had the help in those days of several university students, including medical undergraduates, and other young people, who acted as helpers in a live-in capacity. Those early volunteers included Malcolm Peterson and Helen Anderson (I was later to be the celebrant at their wedding), Marilyn Scott, Jan Davidge, Greg Whiting, Paul and Paula Butler, and Joe Kelleher (now administrator at our Crisis Centre). In those days we were hard up, and these helpers were required to pay board for the privilege of spending much of their free time helping residents and making sure the Home ran well.

The other cost to them was stress. Sometimes they were physically at risk, especially from drunken residents and others who were psychiatrically disturbed. On one occasion Malcolm had asked a seventeen-year-old boy to do his house job. The youth became angry and jumped from the house's top storey on to the roof of the helper's car, causing serious damage.

On another occasion, an eighteen-year-old boy came home the worse for drink and became very aggressive during the evening meal. The youth had been previously completely rejected by his family. He felt this deeply, and when depressed or drinking became totally unreasonable. This particular evening, he started to throw plates around the dining room, firing one at the television set. Next he took to me, because I had tried to restrain him. I followed him out of the room into our courtyard. He turned on me and started throwing empty beer bottles at me. I was caught in a corner, with no escape. Dodging the bottles, I called out to Malcolm to get the police. Eventually the youth ran to the back of the building and threatened to kill himself. The police arrived, we managed to overpower him, and he went into hospital for treatment.

This same youth was later to be a cause of publicity and stress, when he threatened to throw himself off the seventh floor of the partially completed Grafton Nurses' Home. The police rang me to come and help get him down, as he had been asking for me. When I arrived, dusk was setting in and a huge crowd of people had gathered at the scene. Grafton Bridge had been closed off and no traffic was allowed in Park Road, where the building was. Nearby was an ambulance and a fire engine. The police were there in force and anxious to avoid a tragedy. The youth was swaying on a beam high above and shouting at the crowd below.

I asked the police to remain out of sight, as their presence seemed to aggravate the situation and caused him to scream abuse at them, as well as threatening to jump. I also asked that the onlookers be pushed back into neighbouring streets and kept out of sight. The police had wanted the firemen to raise the extended ladder and bring him down. I felt that would precipitate his jumping. The police were uneasy and said I would have to take responsibility for what followed. I started talking to the distraught young man, and gradually climbing up the framework a floor at a time. He responded and kept asking me what the consequences would be if he came down. Slowly he started climbing down as well. There were some scary moments, when he teetered alarmingly on the beam, shouting and causing the crowd to gasp. After much anxiety, we both reached the same landing and the youth reached out to me; putting his arms around me, he sobbed uncontrollably. The drama was over as far as the crowd was concerned, but not for us. As soon as he reached the ground, the police appeared and promptly arrested him. I was in a difficult position, feeling my promises had been set aside. I did all I could to reassure the youth and stayed beside him, going with him in the police car to the psychiatric hospital, where he was detained.

In those days, the drug scene was in its infancy in New Zealand, so this problem only featured occasionally in the referrals to our Home. It was to grow in the mid-1970s onwards, and become a major obstacle to rehabilitating disturbed young people.

Residents in the first few years ranged from sixteen to twenty-five years. Rarely did we have anyone who was attending school. The very first was an Auckland (Boys) Grammar School pupil. (One of our Homes is now sited in the zone area for this much sought-after, academically oriented school.) Now there are over fifty residents attending schools. Another change over the years has been the dramatic drop in the average age of referral from nineteen to fourteen years. The referral population has altered, with more Maori and Polynesian youth requiring residential care. There are more youngsters of single and separated parents seeking help, as the numbers of such families have risen.

Criminal acts and violent behaviour feature much more frequently than was the case in the early years of Youthlink. While the reasons that crime and violence have accelerated in society and among the young are debatable, I believe that fractured family relationships, racial tensions, unemployment for parents and youth, easy access to alcohol, drugs and solvents, failures within the school system, and the constant models for crime and violent reactions to frustration that abound, all have contributed to these social developments.

In our beginnings, we called ourselves the Youthline House Trust. This was to take advantage of the publicity surrounding the Youthline Phone Counselling Service, which I had earlier founded in Auckland, and was chairman of for a number of years. It seemed best to use the same name for organisations that were closely linked in their objectives at that time. The growth of our organisation in recent times, especially with the setting up of a Crisis Centre in 1984, made a name change necessary. The public became confused at times with the phone service and our own

11

project, leading to correspondence, donations and referrals becoming mixed. Philosophically, too, there were some differences, including the association of the phone service with Centrepoint (a controversial community therapeutic living group, which attained notoriety with its free attitudes to sexual expression); this led to rejection of our organisation at times, and withholding of support. A Trustee, Brian Picot, came up with the new name Youthlink.

When the Trust was established in 1971 to operate the new House in Mt Albert, the original members were Professor Cecil Lewis, then Dean of the Auckland Medical School, Margaret Roberts, a former secondary school inspector, Geoffrey Greenbank, former Headmaster of Kings College, and myself. When Geoff attended our first Christmas party at Lloyd Avenue, he was surprised to find that four of the residents were Old Boys of his school, an expensive, single-sex, private school with a religious structure, which claimed excellence in the product of its system. The message was that even children from privileged backgrounds can have severe social and emotional problems like anyone else.

We have been blest in our Trustees both then and since. They have been supportive and encouraging of my ideas, especially the expansion of the project as new needs arose. It had become clear after the first three years of existence that the House in Mt Albert was too small for the numbers seeking admission. The operation at that time was unique in Auckland. Now there are many residential houses for young people; then, ours was the only one of its kind, apart from residential hostels run by some Churches for out-of-town youth studying or apprenticed to various trades, or Maori hostels run for rural youth studying in the city or working there.

Pressure of numbers was not the only problem we faced. The smallness of the site was a difficulty, in that the large two-storeyed house covered nearly the entire small section, leaving no room for outdoor recreation. We were right on top of our neighbours and the strain to keep noise levels down, especially from stereos, was constant.

We began looking for an alternative building; this was to bring about a closer working relationship with the Department of Social Welfare. We approached the Department for some financial assistance in purchasing a property. A suitable house was available in Remuera Road for about $66,000. Officials from Head Office in Wellington flew up and looked at the property; but they informed us that bringing it up to Health and Social Welfare standards would make the cost prohibitive.

It was suggested that we seek a site for a new building through the Department of Lands and Survey, and we could then be given financial assistance to build. So began what was to be years of fruitless searching for a site, and then for permission to build. We were offered a choice of six possible sites belonging to the Crown. The one that best suited our purposes was in Kohimarama, a wealthy Auckland suburb, which then as now had no welfare buildings within its boundaries. We were warned that there might be objections from neighbours. We were amazed to learn that 180 signatories opposed our movement into their area.

The Auckland City Council's Town Planning Committee arranged a hearing, and it became the longest sitting of its kind. I was required to prepare statistics for the hearing: these showed that after nearly four years in operation, we had given a home to 159 youths, 40 females and 119 males. The referral sources, with the numbers that came from then, were as follows: parents (31), hospitals (17), school counsellors (16), self referrals (16), Social Welfare (15), Justice (12), university counsellors (11), general practitioners (11), Youthline phone counsellors (9), church agencies (6), teachers training colleges (5), and other sources (10).

At the time of the hearings there were twenty young people in residence, plus two children under three years of age. A description of their reasons for coming to Lloyd Avenue covered many social and emotional problems, but mostly related to family ruptures. The youngest teenager (fifteen) was an adopted boy; he had been rejected by his father, who was a professional man and constantly put the boy down. A sixteen-year-old came from a situation in which he and his stepfather did not get on, and the boy was seen as a threat to the marriage. Another of the same age had never known his father, and his mother was considered neurotic, her behaviour destabilising the youth. There were four seventeen-year-olds: one, a girl under Social Welfare's care, had been rejected by her parents, was unstable and at that stage, unemployable. Another was a solo mother with a three-month-old baby; she had no parents or relations. Another youth had lived for twelve years in a psychiatric hospital. He was effeminate in his manner, given to thieving, and unable to relate to others. The final seventeen-year-old was the son of an alcoholic father, and his mother claimed she could not control him.

The remaining residents were between nineteen and twenty-five years. Two were from broken homes in which the mother was unable to cope with their behaviour; three were very depressed and unable to relate socially — one of them had been in psychiatric care following her broken relationship; another was a university student with a severe speech impediment and problems in socialising; another was a solo father with a daughter of two years, experiencing pressure in his role and wishing to have female influences in her upbringing. The remainder were there because of trouble with the law, and were in need of a supervised and supportive environment.

Prior to the City Council hearing, we arranged for a public meeting to be held in the Kohimarama Anglican Church Hall. One hundred and thirty-five people attended, mainly local residents, but also the press, Youthline Trust members and some of the Lloyd Avenue residents. On reading over the verbatim record of that meeting ten years later, I was surprised to read that I had intended to keep the Mt Albert House open, as well as the new building.

The issue that most concerned the people objecting to the project expanding into their area did not get voiced publicly at the Hall meeting, or the later hearings. What really bothered people was the threat to property values that our coming might create. This was never openly discussed, and any challenge by our lawyers or myself on that issue was denied. Among the issues that were publicly raised were concerns about wild parties, motor-cycles, and radios echoing down the slopes, disturbing the 'elderly, quiet, residents'; the undesirable types that would be attracted into the neighbourhood; the amount of supervision that might or might not be exercised; drinking problems, thefts, more rubbish bags in the street; the danger to the local primary school children, the cubs (they would not be safe out at night) and the scouts (they would not be able to continue storing the empty bottles in the adjoining school yard). Some residents were concerned that children might be knocked down.

But the 'sleeper' came near the end of the Council hearings, when one resident giving evidence was worried that we might bring homosexuals into the area. My comment was that Kohimarama would be an abnormal area statistically if there were not already homosexuals living there or even perhaps represented in the large sample of objectors to the project. I was required to give a thirty minute dissertation on homosexuality as distinct from paedophilia, which seemed in need of clarification for many of the objectors.

One of our supporters at the Kohimarama meeting said that it had been a gathering that had tried to put me on trial. He also indicated that many of the matters raised were emotional issues and had nothing to do with town planning requirements. Eventually the Town Planning Committee turned our application down and the then Mayor, Sir Dove-Myer Robinson, sought a new hearing.

Clearly the wealth of the objectors would be used to fight against our movement into their neighbourhood. It was suggested that some of the land in Orakei might be a happier prospect, and that would prevent us being entangled for years in court litigation over the Kohimarama site. We did not know the new, even more severe difficulties that were ahead of us in choosing to accept a piece of Crown land at Kupe Street, Orakei — Bastion Point.

The local Marae Community approved of our coming and we began to establish a close working relationship. Had we been able to build there in 1976 as planned, a lot of the racial problems we are presently having to contend with would have been avoided. When the Act of Parliament had been passed giving us a ninety-nine year lease of an acre of land, we were instructed by Government to move rapidly and get the building under way. Working drawings were commissioned from architect Graham Smith. They were never to be put into use. As we were about to raise funds for the project, the now famous sit-in by a section of the Maori community began.

The next notice from Government was that we should desist from any further developments because of the political situation at Bastion Point. Some of the leaders, claiming all the land for the Maori as of right, told me they had no objection to our Trust being on the land, but they insisted that it should be them and not the Crown who donated the land for our purposes.

In the midst of all these wranglings and moves for a fresh home, tragedy struck at Lloyd Avenue, with a devastating fire on the night of Saturday 30 April 1977 caused by a heater in one of the resident's rooms, and possibly by faulty wiring; the House was ablaze in seconds. Fortunately no lives were lost, but the House was a total write off. We were to learn within a few days that a permit would not be granted for a replacement building, given the small section we owned.

For weeks I hunted everywhere for a property to meet our immediate needs, in the hope that our Bastion Point project would soon get under way. While everyone had expensive homes to sell me, no one was willing to shelter the twenty-three residents made homeless by the fire. There were quite a few Catholic Church properties standing empty, but the authorities said they wished to sell them, and our presence in the building might prevent a sale. Shortly afterwards, one of them was made available for Vietnamese refugees. I could not help wondering about 'charity at home'.

After some four weeks of makeshift living we were able to move into a condemned city building in Greys Avenue. The building was vast, and offered most of the residents private rooms. We spent some $20,000 on repairs in order to meet minimal fire and health requirements. The people of Auckland had been generous and responded to a mayoral appeal for us run by the *Auckland Star*.

The Mayor of Auckland at the time, Sir Dove-Myer Robinson, suggested the appeal to replace the building we had lost. He made a press statement:

> As Mayor of the City, I recognise the importance of the work that is being done by Youthline. As you know, Father Donnelly, I've called on you for your assistance in one case of a relative of my own, and also referred many other cases to you. I feel these young people who stay at the Youthline Hostel are in need of companionship. They want to feel wanted and the Hostel meets that need. I'm quite sure that without this facility being available, many of them could become very much isolated and disorientated. They would probably drift away from the community altogether. As far as I am concerned, Youthline is a very valuable social service to the people, not only of the City of Auckland, but to the people of the Greater Auckland Area, and I think everybody should be grateful to you and to those assisting you in what you are doing.

He signed it 'Mayor Robbie of Auckland'.

Some were advising me to call it a day and rest, as I had done enough. But I wanted to carry on. The appeal raised over $150,000, yet we were never able to put that money, as intended at the time, into a replacement building. It has been invested, and the interest over the years has helped pay one and a half salaries. It gradually became clear to the Trust and myself by 1979, that there was little hope of the Bastion Point situation being solved in a way that would benefit our needs. We offered the land back to Government, but that also had its problems. The transfer back is still being negotiated at the time of writing.

The Auckland City Mission who owned the Greys Avenue building required it back for its own purposes. George Gair, then Minister of Social Welfare, saw to it (at very short notice) that we could take over the former dental nurses' home in Almorah Road,

Epsom. We moved into that building on the eve of Christmas, 1979, and have been there ever since.

Shortly after moving in, we were told that some neighbours were organising a petition to prevent our coming into the area. Unbeknown to them, we had already arrived. I do not blame people for feeling anxious at a large number of young people moving into a district, especially when they come from disturbed backgrounds. The fear of the unknown is strong, and many people have had no dealings with the type of youth we are dealing with, and are scared for their safety. It also has to be accepted that even with the closest supervision and the best of intentions, from time to time neighbours will be offended by noise, property damage or suspicion that all crime in the area comes from such a place.

One of the constants in caring for emotionally disturbed youngsters is that at times they will vent their anger inappropriately by smashing windows or bashing in doors and walls. They will sometimes yell out so loudly that their voices carry to the nearby houses; or they will interfere with a neighbour's property, though that is a rare event. Our residents are frequently blamed for all the crimes or problems in the immediate neighbourhood and beyond, though we have frequently been able to establish our innocence in such cases. It is also a fact that our residential Houses have in turn experienced theft, damage and noise from within the neighbourhood. Often we have rubbish dumped on our properties. Most people forget that such properties as ours are also on the receiving end of neighbourhood problems.

The Department of Social Welfare formally offered us the Almorah Road property at a nominal rent, in return for us contracting to take in referrals of State Wards and young people under supervision. They also assisted us with staffing, because as the scheme had grown and more and more referrals were youngsters out of work, and more generally disturbed than had previously been the case, we needed paid staff and more of them. An arrangement was made that we would receive the majority of our staff through the Labour Department's unemployment schemes.

The Department also spent some money on making the house suitable for its new purposes and repairing those parts that were run down. A good deal of interior decorating went on, and the property was brought up to an attractive standard. By 8 November 1981, the building was ready to be officially opened. At the opening of The Glade by George Gair, I stated that this was a very important day for us: after ten years of insecurity, we had a sense of permanency. I said that it had been an ambition of mine for many years to get a place that was adequate for our purposes and would foster the growth of deprived young adolescents. At that time over a thousand had been through our system. I outlined the changes that had taken place over the years, including more sophisticated programmes. We then had ten residents attending school (now it is fifty), and this was a sign of changing times. We also had a mixture of races and ages, and a clear spirit of caring for one another.

It was a joy to have people at that gathering who linked our origins and our present — people such as John Graham, Cecil Lewis, Margaret Roberts, Peter Hillyer, Geoff Greenbank, Brian Picot and Lindo Ferguson. Two, Sir Dove-Myer Robinson and Colin Kay, had been Mayors of Auckland. It was also good to be able to record appreciation of those who had helped run the home and keep its momentum going over the years. These unpaid helpers included Malcolm Peterson, Helen Anderson, Marilyn Scott, Greg Whiting, Paul and Paula Butler, Joe Kelleher, Jan Davidge, Carolyn Keats, Cheryl Eyre, Cheryl Smith and Warren Sattler.

The residents felt a deep sense of belonging and some awe at the attendance of so many notables. They commented on feeling part of the history of the place, and went out of their way to make visitors welcome by serving them afternoon tea. It was one of the highlights in our history, and I personally felt that at last we had 'arrived'.

By this time I had been involved for over ten years in the running of the House, and had spent most of my days living with the residents. I was beginning to feel the personal toll on my health, especially as I had a number of demanding irons in the fire at the time. Besides running the House and overseeing the care of the residents and staff, I had a full-time teaching position at the Medical School, and was broadcasting on Radio Pacific four nights and part of Sunday each week. It was hard to catch up on missed sleep.

So I moved out of The Glade, and have lived in a nearby flat ever since. One of my reasons in moving was to give more autonomy to Cheryl Smith, who was in charge of the House, assisted by Warren Sattler. It seemed important for the survival of the project that others assume administrative responsibilities. My role became more supervisory, rather than being involved in the day-to-day management. I missed the immediacy of contact with the residents and almost felt puzzled at myself, knowing that I had moved away from a living situation that had been my dream for so many years in the past. But then and now, I believe it was the right decision. The whole Trust has benefited from others sharing in the various roles that once been almost exclusively mine.

During this period we placed a greater emphasis than before on the structures and programmes that we painstakingly devised. These are described in Chapter 5. In addition we began to get much younger referrals, going as low as nine years of age. With a much broader age group to cater for, it became necessary to introduce more regulations and a tighter structure. One of the benefits of moving to The Glade was distancing ourselves from the Queen Street hotels, whose proximity had been a major problem in the Greys Avenue days. The building was a gracious one, and this improved environment affected and modified the residents' behaviour. Attractive surroundings make a major difference to young people's responses and the degree of care they show for themselves and their property.

Numbers remained at about forty, from an earlier ceiling of twenty-eight, yet we were turning away about ten referrals a week. It seemed clear that there was a need for an extension into another building. We envisaged placing older youth in the new premises. So the search began. It might be possible to get a property at St Georges Bay Road, Parnell, previously used as a youth periodic detention centre. The Justice Department was closing down such centres, and this one had become available.

Unbeknown to our Trust, Odyssey, a drug rehabilitation residential programme, was also after the property, which would have housed forty residents. Communication was not good, and while we were negotiating and things seemed promising, we read in the daily press that the Government had given the building to Odyssey. This was a shock, not because we did not value the therapy programme Odyssey was running, but because we had thought the place was virtually ours.

Letters passed to and fro, and eventually we were told that another former periodic detention centre was available in Mt Roskill. At the last minute it looked as if another group might beat us to that site as well — they were negotiating privately with the Prime Minister, Sir Robert Muldoon. But we were informed by the Minister of Justice, Mr Jim McLay, that the property was available to us for a peppercorn rental. Mr Graham Armstrong, Head Probation Officer, had facilitated the transfer of the property, assisted by the goodwill of Mr Murray Hay, Auckland Senior Probation Officer.

My brother Kevin, who had been studying for a doctorate in psychology in Michigan, USA, had moved back to New Zealand with his wife and children and had been working at The Glade while negotiations were proceeding. We were later to appoint him to be the first Administrator of the new Home at Mt Roskill, called Rowan House. However, before that could happen, we had to go through the anxiety of obtaining approval from the Mt Roskill Borough Council for the right to use the site for residential purposes. I was required to appear before the Council, who had circularised the neighbours to find out if there were any objections to our proposal.

Prior to this hearing, we had invited all interested neighbours to the House and talked over with them what we intended to do. They appeared very reasonable, expressed their fears, and sought certain reassurances. Eventually a licence was granted to begin the project. It began operating on 25 October 1982, under the temporary leadership of Diana Foster, who had worked for some years at The Glade.

It cost around $33,000 to set up the new Home. Alterations were made to provide more privacy and furnishings, and meeting the fire and health requirements proved expensive. Rowan House was officially opened by the then Minister of Justice, Jim McLay, on Sunday 8 May 1983. By this time my brother had returned to America, and Cheryl Smith took over the administration.

The property has a small house alongside the larger one, and for a time we experimented with its use. Initially it was an assessment centre, where residents were prepared for moving into one of the larger Houses. Later we tried putting the maturer and more responsible residents in it to learn independent living skills prior to leaving altogether. None of the schemes worked, mainly because of the proximity of the two buildings to each other, and hence a 'contamination' factor. Now it is a family home for younger children.

Staffing was another problem. We lacked funds to pay suitable people to fill all the positions. In fact, it was becoming increasingly obvious that our resources for providing the mature staff we needed were totally inadequate. We had relied for some years on the unemployment schemes sponsored by the Labour Department, who paid salaries for out-of-work adults to receive training for future permanent employment. Hour after hour was spent writing up job descriptions, negotiating with the Labour Department and trying to work with the inexperience of such a large proportion of the staff. While there were some excellent people who came to work for us, we had to let most of these go at the end of their year's term with us, because we lacked staff funding. As the job market improved after the Labour Government came to power in 1984, the numbers, variety and maturity of unemployed went down.

Despite these problems, we battled on and the projects grew. At the same time as we were establishing Rowan House, an opportunity arose to set up our own school programme for some residents. As the numbers of referrals of younger residents increased, we found that many of these had learning problems as well as difficulties with ordinary schools. It was evident that youngsters who were emotionally disturbed, and who had just moved into a totally new environment, often with considerable grief over separation from their families, needed time before other changes were made, including a new outside school. We found that placing new admissions or even longer term residents into an outside school was often a path to failure. They tried the resources of the secondary school and often brought out its limitations, including the coping skills of a few staff. It has become increasingly evident, that secondary schools are less able to deal with demanding, violent, rebellious or disturbed youth than was previously the case. Part of this has to do with the increase in numbers and intensity of such cases, the rest with a lack of training for teachers in coping with maladjusted youth and a lack of flexibility of schools to meet these special needs.

With help from educational sources, we were able to operate a private school programme from The Glade. It is a classroom extension from nearby St Peters College, Epsom. While we built a classroom, the school operated from a disused room belonging to the nearby Mater Hospital. After several months The Glade School was ready, and was opened informally on 12 May 1983. One of the important people at that gathering was Dick Oliver, then involved with Special Education, who made its establishment possible.

The school has been a great asset to the work of the Trust. It has enabled some young people who would otherwise have been put off education for life to make a new discovery of learning and their own skills. So many had a fear of exposure of their inadequacies in front of others in the usual classroom that they had given away any attempt to carry on with their schooling. They reported having felt a failure in its systems, and loathed its seeming rigidity and irrelevance to their needs.

The school operates somewhat differently to the usual secondary system. Pupils fit into two categories: those who are out to achieve some attainment through the examination system (e.g. School Certificate), and those who function best in a creative,

21

activity based programme. Recently the McKenzie Trust, assisted by an anonymous donation, has helped fund the building of a hall, to serve alongside the present classroom as a general utility building, as well as a gymnasium for all.

Our aim has been to make The Glade School a place of transition, with the purpose of helping young people return to normal classrooms where possible. It has been our experience that some residents will never be able to cope with the less personalised nature of the larger secondary school; for them this school is a permanent placement. With two teachers in attendance, we are able to cater for about sixteen residents. The policy has been to get the school to function as a group, with the teachers using the co-operation of the pupils in planning, discipline and activities.

In 1982 Dr Fraser MacDonald, then Superintendent of Carrington Hospital, called a meeting of all those interested in the direction and improvement of youth services in Auckland. Some forty people attended, and so was begun the Adolescent Forum, which still operates. At that meeting many people from South Auckland, as well as the Central City, spoke of their concerns for the young. One of the most vocal was the Police Department, which wanted more agencies to assist in the placement of rejected, problem or homeless youth.

Many ideas were put forward as solutions to the problems. I came up with one idea I had been dwelling on for quite some time. That was to set up a centre to which the young and their parents could come for support and guidance in times of problems. Much of my concern resulted from years of working with so many youngsters who had multiple placements after coming into care. Some had as many as twenty foster experiences within a couple of years. I believed it was necessary for some agency to co-ordinate such a young person's placement, to ensure that a proper assessment was made, and to see an ongoing evaluation or check of what was happening occurred.

The Adolescent Forum then, and through the next two and a half years, supported that proposal and made submissions to Government to get the Centre established. While the enthusiasm was keen within the Forum, cold winds blew against it outside. There was suspicion within the Maori and Island communities that this was another white takeover of resources. For the next few years I drafted many a proposal, making amendments and incorporating changes that seemed to be required if the idea was to get anywhere. I visited many communities in Central and South Auckland, besides talking with those involved in youth work, many on a voluntary basis.

Visits to Government officers seemed to get me nowhere. In desperation I sought an appointment with the then Minister of Social Welfare, Venn Young. There seemed to be something missing. At length it became clear that I had to produce evidence of local community support, or I would never get the Centre off the ground. The three sources that proved of most help, and whose co-operation eventually made the project possible, were the Auckland Hospital Board, the Presbyterian Social Services and a Mt Albert community-based religious group, the Muriel Kerr-Taylor Trust.

After much negotiating, the Hospital Board promised to fund a psychiatric nurse for the Centre. They were later to offer help in acquiring premises. The Chairman of our Trust, Dr Lindo Ferguson, had to telephone the Hospital Executive in Melbourne, where they were attending a conference, to get an urgently required letter of intent to give to Government. The Presbyterian Services Support Group promised us a part-time (two days a week) staff member to assist in family therapy. The Kerr-Taylor Trust had for a number of years debated an appropriate use of its house and land at Mt Albert. After hearing of my project, and a number of meetings, they agreed to allow their property to be used for the Centre.

The plans to get the Kerr-Taylor Trust involved nearly went disastrously wrong. This group of elected representatives of the major Churches in Mt Albert had come one evening to The Glade to hear from the Youthlink Trust about the project, and to make a final decision regarding their involvement. But the residents at The Glade had a plot of their own.

A few days previously, five of the residents had been involved in a fight near Newmarket with some schoolboys. There had been an angry reaction from The Glade's administration regarding their behaviour and the disgrace they had brought on us. Someone spread the rumour that all these distinguished-looking visitors had come to close the property down. So three of the residents lined up the fire hose to give the 'enemy' a wet reception. It was lucky for their future and that of the Crisis Centre that an alert staff member saw them hovering outside the window of the room we were meeting in, and put a stop to their scheme. The nozzle of the fire hose was going to be inserted through the open window, and the visitors hosed. How they believed such an action would in any way save their home remains to this day a mystery. Fortunately, the guests left without any knowledge of how close they were to a drenching!

When all the necessary promises were gathered, Dr Ferguson,

Brian Picot and I sought time with the Minister, who was visiting Auckland but had a very tight schedule. He kindly fitted us into his breakfast session at the Hyatt Kingsgate Hotel before he caught his plane for Wellington. All seemed promising, and the final proposal, in the form of a fifteen-page booklet, was working its way to his desk through the Head Office of the Department of Social Welfare.

Suddenly, as it was about to be signed by the Minister, Sir Robert Muldoon called a snap election and our project seemed in danger. There was no possibility of a new project being approved while the country was in the throes of a general election. The weeks went by, a new Government was elected, and our proposal was back to the drawing board. In anticipation of Mr Young's signing approval I had planned to make a quick three week visit to the States, England and Europe to study Crisis Centres in those countries. The only time I could take from my University teaching was in August. The election had delayed approval. But with faith in the new Minister, I went on the trip and gained valuable information and confidence in the project. The most important relearning was from youth services I saw in Belgium, France and Italy, which stressed the need to be supportive and involving of the adolescent's family in a non-blaming way. These seemed to be the techniques used in Europe, plus an expectation that families would be involved in therapy, rather than that they wouldn't.

A few days after my return to Auckland in September 1984, the new Minister of Social Welfare, Ann Hercus, announced that the Government was funding the project in terms of three salaries. We were delighted with the news. One of the conditions was an immediate start to the project, by the employment of permanent staff. So we advertised and extensively interviewed for the right people. Those eventually appointed included a family therapist, a youth counsellor, and a Maori social worker.

The next problem was to find a suitable base to work from. The Kerr-Taylor House at Mt Albert was undergoing extensive renovations, and the delays meant it was several months off being ready. Once again the Mater Hospital was helpful, and we had the use of some rooms in an adjoining building for a month. Then, still without a base, and not sure what the Hospital Board's position was regarding provision of rooms, we accepted an offer to use some disused rooms at Carrington Hospital.

Several difficulties were involved in this move. One was a stigma for youths using a centre so closely associated with a mental hospital. The other was the inaccessibility of the site.

However, we were grateful for any base to work from, and used it for the next four months. In the meantime I continued to negotiate with Hospital Board officials about a more suitable site. The Greenlane Nurses' Home seemed a possibility, but that came to nothing. Then the Director of the Adolescent Unit of the Auckland Hospital moved into Marinoto in Symonds Street with the Child Health Team there.

We had worked closely with the Adolescent Unit ever since Dr Muriel Taylor of America set it up during a year's stay in this country. Meeting with our staff weekly, she had provided immensely helpful guidance on our more difficult residents. When she left, her successor, Dr Peter McGeorge continued the same support. He suggested we might be able to convert the disused basement into workable premises.

After further negotiations, we obtained approval to share the Marinoto building. Several working bees cleared out the rubbish and rot of fifteen years of disuse, and we moved in. The Board kindly assisted with the repair of several roofs and the painting. A generous carpenter, Joe Manuel, put up partitions and made rooms habitable. After some weeks of functioning, on 7 August 1985, we had an informal 'opening'.

The development of the Mt Albert base for the Crisis Centre had dragged on interminably. Part of the problem was raising funds, over and above what had been paid out to purchase the original property, to carry out renovations and extensions. It had originally been intended to operate the whole Centre, interviews and accommodation from that base. While we waited for the building to be made ready, I had tried to obtain temporary use of a property belonging to the Justice Department in Violet Street, Mt Albert. Neighbours objected to having anything psychological or psychiatric going on in their area, and blocked the move.

It was at this stage that I approached the Hospital Board, and saw Dr L. Honeyman and Ian Campbell for help in obtaining accommodation. It was also made clear to us that the Mt Albert Council would not allow counselling or interviewing referrals at the Kerr-Taylor House. Once we had obtained premises through the Hospital Board, there was less pressure to get the Mt Albert Emergency Accommodation completed. An upstairs section had been added as a flat for live-in staff, and the downstairs area greatly improved.

The Muriel Kerr-Taylor Trust invited Ann Hercus, Minister of Social Welfare, to open the House on 18 August 1985. She had a special interest in the occasion because her Department had helped make available to the Kerr-Taylor Trust some funds from lottery

25

sources. In her address, the Minister mentioned the uniqueness of the project, in that it represented a combination of the resources and interests of many sections of the community, besides the Government input.

Mrs Hercus said her stipulation for Government help had been that the project reflected the involvement of agencies additional to Youthlink, so that it meant there was a clear belief in the need for such a service; and this had been proven in a particularly successful way. The Minister went on to say:

> There are many, many parents and young people that have benefited from the time and effort made available for them by Father Donnelly and his staff. However, equally important from my point of view is the close working relationship that exists between Youthlink and the Department of Social Welfare. For instance, it is estimated that over half the young people at The Glade or Rowan House at any one point in time are either in the care of the Department or have been referred by their Social Workers. This was done, not so much because the Department lacks its own facilities, but because of our recognition of the unique programme offered by Youthlink. My Department does not have, nor want to have a monopoly of brilliant social services in the country. I was pleased to approve a special package of funding assistance for the Adolescent Assessment Centre.

During the rest of her speech, Mrs Hercus mentioned her awareness that organisations like ours were having special difficulties taking on staff, given the changing nature of unemployment schemes. She promised a willingness to help overcome such problems. Prior to that announcement, and unaware of such support, the Chairman of the Trust, Dr Ferguson, had invited Mrs Hercus to visit Rowan House on her way to the airport, to discuss with us our financial concerns, especially with regard to adequate staffing.

Cheryl Smith, Dr Ferguson and I had a pleasant meeting with Mrs Hercus and her secretary. I found her quick to grasp the point of our problem, searching in her questions, and clear as to what she could do to help us. In fact, everything that she promised to do for us that Sunday afternoon was meticulously carried out.

The Voluntary Organisation Training Programme was our major source of funding for salaries. We had been rapidly getting into overdraft, since positions under these schemes were not being replaced as they fell vacant. This meant the Trust, which had to have the staff to care for the young, was being forced to pay from its own limited funds. Mrs Hercus, as she had indicated in her speech, appreciated that we were one of the major referral places for State Wards or youth under temporary care by the Department of Social Welfare.

Assessments began by the Department and our position was rationalised. It had become very clear to us that if caring for the needy young was to be well done, we had to be free to employ people from a workforce wider and more experienced than that generally offered through unemployment schemes. Toward the end of 1985, word came through that a funding system had been approved enabling us to continue our work. It meant that Mrs Hercus and her Department had regularised payments without us having to negotiate through a variety of sources. This meant a greater accountability for our service, but that was something I was happy to accept.

When this news came through I shared it with some who had been involved with me in my visionary days of 1971, when I first set up a home for needy youth. Like them I found it difficult to match our efforts then, with no funding, scant resources and little recognition with the multi-faceted service operating today. A staff of thirty-two, over eighty residents, a school and a rehabilitation programme for employment, as well as a service for the wider community with problems, would have been incomprehensible to me fifteen years ago. But they had all come about.

Some may envy the assets that are presently ours. But they have been earned and are maintained at enormous cost of stress and ingenuity. They are the fruits of many people's faith and generosity, and long hours of voluntary service or overtime that have never been financially rewarded. I made a commitment to the whole project by leaving full-time work at the Medical School in 1985.

Any success that Youthlink has had has grown out of the belief in the project by those who have given much time and support to it. The staff of many years have made it successful and helped it spread. If we have grown too quickly, it was because the opportunities were there and had to be grasped. Now is a time for consolidation and a search for excellence. In that quest, as in the whole story of Youthlink's development, the most important people are the recipients of the service, who have had faith enough to allow its interventions in their lives.

(2)
A Basis for Caring

I don't think you will remember me, but I stayed at Rowan House for several months. Before I started this letter I was going to ring you up so that I could see you sometime, but I don't want to take up too much of your spare time as I know you are really busy. Then I thought I'd let you know how I was getting on, but you probably can't really remember me, my situation and all that, so I will spare you!

What I really want to say is a genuine thank you for the help you gave me when I needed it. Before we met we were total strangers but as soon as you heard of my situation you treated me like a son and I really appreciated that. I go over to Rowan House now and then to see Joe and I think you are all doing one hell of a job. I don't want to sound as though I'm trying to patronise you or anything phoney like that. . . . I'm a pretty cynical person, I guess, but you opened my eyes a lot. That place sure isn't like home, but at least it's somewhere and I can tell people in it are grateful. If I was a bit wealthier I'd give you a big sum of money, but I can't afford that . . . and if you do remember me, remember me as a friend.

Yes, I remembered Paul and was moved by the full kindness and appreciation of his letter. He had found it difficult facing the discipline of living with a lot of other youths, but he had stuck with it. I believe he had sensed what is basic to all our work — we cared.

Not all residents leave our Homes with a sense of gratitude or appreciation for what has been attempted. Sometimes this comes later, sometimes not at all. Ray was an unhappy youth at The Glade. His relationships with his parents were strained and as far as his father was concerned, non-existent. The man had no contact with his sixteen-year-old and despite every effort of Ray to win acceptance, there was no response. Worse still was the fact that the father, a university graduate and practising in a supposedly caring profession, had used mental and physical torture on his son during the years the boy had lived at home.

While at The Glade, Ray never seemed to respond to any caring initiatives. He reacted by distancing himself from staff and other residents by joining a punk rock group. He was into all their negativity in the form of abuse of alcohol, baiting of blacks, anti-authority statements and contempt for life. His schooling suffered, and he constantly flouted attempts at discipline. But there was a clear softer side to Ray, which in some moments of relaxation emerged.

Eventually he ran away from the House and there was little we could do. I wrote to his address telling him that support was always available. No reply. I heard of his criminal and drug behaviours. On one occasion, when he was in intensive care, Warren Sattler and myself spent some hours at his bedside as he struggled between life and death. He became so violent in the recuperative stages (as he reacted to drug withdrawal), that he was placed in a locked, unfurnished room with only a bed on the floor. On recovery, he returned to his old group and former ways.

It was a neat surprise earlier this year, when I was announced in Dunedin as giving an open address in the Octagon Square, to meet up with Ray. He was working through therapy, and hearing I was speaking, had travelled some 24 km to meet me. He was warm and positive about his future as he struggled to move away from the ties of the past. We walked together and talked for forty minutes or so. I later wrote saying how good I felt about the steps he was taking and the courage he was showing. He replied, speaking positively of my work and the stands I took.

Never let this negative, suppressive society of homophobics, violent ignoramuses drag you down, like it did with me. But now I'm on my 'journey' coming up and God help me, nothing is going to drag me back. Circumstance really led me through some dark and lonely roads. I am gonna come out on top like you said, and I will find that content, peaceful, full state of ultimate happiness in life.

My bloody battle for change has been a tough experience. Not a great deal in terms of tangible changes have occurred, but at least I am on the road. It took me nineteen years to build this pile up of mental pollution, so it's gonna take a lot longer than my stay here for now four months. . . . Suicide now seems such a waste, but it becomes such an obsession when you are living a life that's a waste.

My doctor wrote to my father a couple of months ago. We have not had any contact whatsoever for five years. There was no reply. He rang him overseas. He was not in agreement at any further contact. My father has his problems. I can accept that. We will meet again in life though; I'm going to make sure — he can't break the link of father and son that easily. I have finally met a totally compatible girl, whom I feel a lot of unselfish love for. So maybe if I ever have a son I could turn up on my father's steps and say 'You are a grandfather'. That would make him feel something.

I can see the past as something necessary to create a future. Meaning the past tortuous life I can learn from and accept and heed as a warning to not let myself be overwhelmed by circumstances created by loneliness, anger, misunderstanding, sorrow, fear. Instead I will plan a balanced well-thought out life, applying my intelligence, creativity and a hunger for happiness. . . . All those hateful, rebellious days at The Glade, I didn't see it or really know you. I was blinded by my rebellious nature. As I said back then though — I think to feel an understanding for life, you have to experience it yourself and learn the hard way practically. Oh boy, have I learnt. But there is still a whole life ahead of me, of learning and it's gonna have its ups and downs; but it's gonna be generally up and up. Think positively, I do. One day we shall meet again I promise.

That letter is the kind of response that makes so much of the years of energy in trying to help a youth really rewarding.

Not all residents are able to talk out their leaving. Joyce left a note that read, 'I thought I should let you know of my intention to leave the "House" this weekend. I'm sorry you were out tonight so I couldn't explain things to you, but I'll see you tomorrow. I hope I have your understanding and approval. I'd hate to leave without it. Thanks for the help and friendship I've found here.'

Then there are the residents who have left the House very rebellious at its restrictions or feeling somehow unwelcome. Quite a number wish to return, on reflection, and complete those things they originally set out to achieve. Peter wrote me a letter I could not resist.

How's life. Things are pretty good for me, apart from a few family problems, that you probably know all about. Dad thinks I should go back to living at The Glade. He thinks I was better off living there with you, and the rest of my friends that are there. I am homesick and I want to live there with you all again. I'll be an angle (sic). I'll go to school and do anything you want me to. Just please say yes. Can you ring me as soon as possible. If I do come back do promise me that you will not let anyone take me away. Please, please promise me. Please ring back as soon as possible. Please hurry. Longing to hear from you.

What is it that makes former residents write in such a way? This is a hard question to answer with any accuracy. I would like to think that the reason above all others was that they felt cared for, respected and loved overall during the time of their stay.

While most former residents eventually respond at later meetings in a friendly and even appreciative way, there are some who hold resentment for years. I have had the experience of being rung and blasted by several ex-residents, when they had a bit too much to drink, and severely abused for ever allowing them to be placed in one of our Houses. The complaint was either over the nature of the people they had to live with, or the stigma they felt they had incurred. Such accusations out of the blue come as a real jolt and can be upsetting.

Sometimes one passes former residents in the street, and they have clearly not wanted to be recognised by me, but the majority are warm and friendly. Recently I heard that a youth who had lived with us several years previously had gone into hospital for an operation. I visited him in his ward the day after it took place. He was reading a newspaper, and after unsmilingly greeting me, continued to read. I decided to ignore that reaction and talked on. Gradually he warmed to me and was friendly and sharing. His initial almost rude response was probably partly embarrassment about his operation and partly shyness after a long interval. He had been rather cross when he left after living with us for many years. When I said goodbye at the hospital, he gave me a warm hug.

From the research literature, experience, and listening to and observing young people and their families, some assumptions have been made within the Youthlink Trust that are a basis for many of the strategies and interventions used in our work. The main ones can be summarised briefly in statements:

- Adolescence is a time of becoming, and is not a fixed state. It is an opportunity to resolve some things that may have been missed out on in earlier years, such as learning closeness and separateness, trust and self control.
- Most parents do love their children, natural or adopted, though they may have hurts or obstacles to expressing this openly and affectionately.
- Young people who have been seriously emotionally, physically or sexually abused need patient management, time to heal and become secure, and can be expected to show a good deal of negativism.
- The young respond to those whom they believe genuinely care for them, clarify boundaries for them, are consistent, and treat them with respect and affirm them.
- Problem behaviour is often an indirect way of trying to resolve inner conflict and can be the acting out of inner pain, confusion or conflict.
- Youth will react better to positive rather than negative statements or requests.

31

- Youth need opportunities to test themselves, as well as to have their legitimate needs met. They need heaps of encouragement.
- The young have rights, which require respecting. These include the right to be heard, to be consulted in matters affecting their lives, to have their opinions treated with attention, to be informed of the basis for decisions made regarding them, and to be treated with dignity. The young respond to information that helps them cope with life.
- They have a need to be given a degree of independence, and their need to feel responsible has to be understood by adults, especially authority figures in their lives. Passivity or conformity are not what make for healthy development; conformity is part of living, but must be treated with great care, so that it is not excessive.
- The young seek attention, and will often use negative or criminal behaviour to that end.
- Recreation, sport and exercise are valuable sources of growth, helping overcome personal problems, and promoting introspection, decision-making and social relating skills.
- Deprived and disadvantaged young persons have a low sense of self-worth, often seeing themselves as irredeemable failures.
- It is important not to respond to symptoms only (e.g. glue-sniffing) in dealing with problem youth, but to uncover the deeper issues behind such behaviour, such as family issues.

These assumptions will feature throughout this book as some of the key factors in our development of philosophy and practice in Youthlink. They are clearly spelt out in our Staff Manual, where the introduction includes this statement:

> The philosophy of the Trust is that anyone who seeks our help is worthy of treatment with dignity and affection. Our care is based on a willingness to see beyond outward appearances and behaviours into the positive features of an individual. We see each referral as a member of a family group of some kind, and we endeavour to work within such a framework and as far as possible with those links.

However, spelling out a philosophy is less difficult than following it through in practice. Any person, but especially disturbed or rejected young people, can be devastatingly accurate in the hurts they throw at those trying to care for them, or having some authority over them. They blatantly ask to be rejected by the person who is initially full of goodwill toward them. The abuse and epithets can be choice. They make accusations, pick on individual weaknesses and unerringly single out your Achilles' heel. It is not only a testing of whether you too will reject them, but a genuine frustration with all you stand for, according to their experience of adults, and a way to confirm that they are basically unlovable.

Michael was an example of a person who made it very difficult for me to be true to the ideals of the philosophy in all its applications. At times he could be quite charming, but at others he would try to push every button possible to achieve rejection. One evening he stood at the entrance to The Glade hurling abuse at any staff who came near him. What was even more disturbing was that he held a carving knife in his hand and was threatening to use it. Something had disturbed him, not least, I believe, the cannabis he had been smoking that day.

Drawn by the commotion, I came out of a meeting to calm him down. When I came near his anger and the decibels expressing it noticeably rose. He told me and all who cared to listen how much he hated me and my f...ing house. He told me how much damage I was doing to people, how there was no love at all in the place, how weak and gutless I was, how inadequate all the staff were, and that above all he would really love to kill me.

I struggled to stay calm and not to buy into his anger and the hurts he was throwing at me. In the meantime, I tried to get rid of the peer group audience that had gathered with some awe, and certainly with much excitement, to witness this confrontation with 'the Boss'. I talked calmly to him, repeatedly telling Michael that I did love him and that I was sad to see his clear distress. My voice was quiet and I tried to calm him. After a period he yelled at me. 'I hate you! I hate you! Stop that f...ing soothing calming talk. Come on, say what you think. I know you f...ing hate me. Go on, say it, say it!'

Eventually, I realised that the fight had gone out of him, even though the abuse and threats were still flowing. Next day he eyed me wryly, I called him into a room and we talked standing up. I told him that I really did care for and love him. But I also expressed my hurt at what he had said the previous evening and asked what was behind it all. He shared his frustrations and above all his sense of being a failure. He ended by putting his arms around me. There had been tears in my eyes through the meeting and I knew that Michael was also moved by what had happened.

But it did not end there. He said as I was about to leave the room, 'I cannot understand you. I have abused you; I have let down the house; I have often stolen from you and smashed your car, and you still say you love me. You're weird!' It is easy to understand, given their past experiences, how some youths behave aggressively, almost at times with contempt, toward those endeavouring to help them. But an approach to them that is consistent, requires consequences for behaviour, is non-violent, takes into account the position or background from which the individual is coming, brings out that person's strengths, and has a degree of warmth and gentleness, in my experience is bound to bring about changes in attitude and behaviour.

There are some who would believe that it is only from a Christian foundation that caring or a philosophy of respect and forgiveness can develop. I do not believe that any one religious source has a monopoly on motivation or selfless giving. Unconditional love is broad in its origins, and no one institution's prerogative. I would like to think that our approach to the young is a manifestation of such love.

Is that approach always experienced by youth or practised by staff? The reality is that it is not. This is a sign of the very difficult nature of this form of caring. Unconditional love means the acceptance of a person for their own sake as a human being, for what they are, not for what they might become. Much of our love in life is conditional upon the responses to our giving, and what we receive back in return. We constantly evaluate the extent to which we will continue to be involved, according to the degree of good vibes or appreciation we experience.

Unconditional love is most difficult to practise when what we do is thrown back in our face, or we find deceit, or trust broken. There are times when we think that our love is honest, but in reality it is mixed with the desire to succeed with an individual, achieve through them or be valued in return. It takes considerable insight and a measure of humility to recognise those limitations and to do something about them.

The people most expected to practise unconditional love are parents. They are often meant to epitomise this form of giving. But this is a rare quality in parenting — to be able to allow freedoms of choice, opportunities to experiment and to express individuality of personality, personal challenges, and still keep on loving the person, without putting conditions on that love. We often express these limitations on our loving by comments such as 'Why can't you be like your sister?'; or 'If you do what I say (or pass that exam) I'll get you that present or let you go on that trip'; or 'Until you apologise, I will have nothing to do with you'; or 'If any son of mine was gay, I'd wish he had never been born'.

An essential element of unconditionally loving a person is

listening to them and, in order to make sure you really hear them, setting aside your own prejudices and needs. This calls for a deep awareness of your personal limitations and needs, then not allowing these to predominate in communication with others seeking your acceptance or care. The ways in which our unfulfilled wants obtrude in caring situations are multiple. A few hypothetical examples illustrate this.

I want a girl to go back to school, so I come to a meeting with her intent on that as the only outcome of our discussion. So I pay scant attention to her objections or difficulties about continuing with school. There is a dismissal of her problems as I try to push my reasons without any real acknowledgement of her needs. She leaves the interview feeling unheard and resentful. Or a social worker from an outside agency is involved in a re-planning for a boy who has recently been caught car converting. The worker suggests that a change of environment from The Glade would be a good idea. My need is not to seem a failure with this youth, so without much thought for the good of the boy, I push for his staying in our Home.

Some believe that unconditional loving is impossible. I don't accept that. It is a difficult quality to achieve in one's loving, and certainly is vital in working with socially and emotionally damaged people. It is well summed up in Paul's letter to the Corinthians when he wrote, 'Love is always patient and kind; it is never jealous; love is never boastful or conceited; it is never rude or selfish; it does not take offence and is not resentful. Love takes no pleasure in other people's failings, but delights in the truth; it is always ready to excuse, to trust, to hope and to endure whatever comes' (1 Cor. 13, 4–7).

So much for the philosophy of caring; in practice it is not easy. Helpers as well as the helped have their limitations, and often a young person's hurt or problems can trigger off unresolved issues in the adult. This can become a barrier to helping effectively the youth in need. The young person who comes into the care of someone other than their parents has his or her own struggles to cope with. Often it is a case of whether to continue existing or making any effort at self-help, because of a previous sense of failure.

How does the philosophy of the Youthlink Trust or similar organisations impinge on young people's lives? Certainly not always successfully. Sometimes, because of expectations not met, the hurt of having personal items stolen, inappropriate handling, occasional neglect by staff, or unwillingness of a given resident to trust those who offer assistance, the experience of residential care

35

can, at least initially, appear a negative one. Often in youth work the rewards are not immediate; so when they come, they help raise the workers' spirits.

Letters, phone calls or visits are always welcome from former residents of the Houses. One which came recently I shared with the present residents of the major Houses. It interests them to hear from people who have moved on from the point they are presently at, and who feel they have achieved something of value.

I am sorry I haven't kept in touch, but every time I settle down to write a few words, something happens to distract me. I miss all the staff, but particularly Warren and Cheryl. I sometimes wonder what I ever would have done without you all to help.

You will be pleased to know I am now a responsible member of the community. I attend a Technical Institute five hours a day, and then work from 6 to 9.30 pm. I am taking a secretarial course, which is a year's work crammed into twelve weeks. So you can imagine how hard we have to work! But it is good to be using the ole gray matter again. . . .
And to top it all off I am back home. I came back at the beginning of August, and I haven't had one serious disagreement with my parents since I shifted back in. In fact, my parents have been so wonderful and supportive that it all seems like a dream. I have come to realise just how wonderful a good parent-child relationship can be, and just how I really do love them. My brother and sister have also become easier to live with. . . . Holding my temper has helped too.

That's all for the moment, but I would love to hear from you some time, even though you are awfully busy. Please say hello to all the other staff for me, and give Warren and Cheryl my best wishes in particular. Lots of loving thoughts, Mary.

It was tremendous to read of the movement over several years of this now twenty-year-old, from a person lacking in confidence, fairly angry with the world and feeling rejected, to a positive, confident and at peace young person. What was especially good was her willingness to pause and thank those who, among others, had helped her to that position.

Another younger girl wrote to Warren, then administrator of The Glade, shortly after she had moved back to relations in the South Island. 'I arrived back in Christchurch in safe hands. My Auntie was really glad to see me, and so was I, her. She enjoys me around here. I want to thank you and Bill (family therapist) for the help you gave me in many things. Also Felix for letting me stay at The Glade, and meeting people, of my own age and older. I hope you all understand that it isn't easy to make a new start like I have, and be happy with it. I am just proving that I can do things without people on my back all the time. . . . There isn't much to do around here, but I am really happy that I'm here. What else can I say except that I'm enjoying myself, but I miss a lot of the people at The Glade. I don't want to mention any names because there are so many of them. I am trying hard to stay out of trouble, like drugs. I know there is no fun in sniffing glue or popping pills . . .'

Behind these letters and many others that could be quoted are some very great efforts on the part of the young writer and those who aided in making changes. There is no magic formula or one approach more than others that brings about the alterations in attitude and life-style which gives peace to the young person and comfort to the family. The same approaches that can be successful with one can fail with another.

Dan was a resident at the original House in Mt Albert who never quite found the peace that came to some other residents. He was a sensitive youth of twenty when he first came to stay at Lloyd Avenue. Insightful and kindly, Dan was an asset to the place and could be relied on for stability in the House. At times he had his moments of uncontrollable depression, which he thought were inherited. He was aware of a loving, supportive family, though his father had been incapacitated for many years, to the point of being a permanent invalid.

Dan was tortured by the way he saw life and the perspective that others brought to it. He had come to us from a psychiatric hospital and had a great deal of resentment about the labelling process he felt he had been through. He often asked 'Who are the real crazies?' He did not believe they were all inside mental institutions, or even that many of those inside deserved to be there. He felt 'the real crazies' were outside such places and showed their craziness by the way they lived and their exploitation of people.

In his moments of unusual behaviour, which seemed to come cyclically, he was never violent and made sense if one listened carefully. He kept in touch after leaving the House. Mostly I heard from him when things were proving difficult or he wanted to talk over some proposed course of action.

On one occasion I was phoned by a duty solicitor asking if I would assist Dan in court as he was up on a disorderly behaviour charge, allegedly having threatened some people. I visited Dan in the cells and found him dressed in a Batman suit — cape and all. The story emerged that he had been working as a gardener at a private girls' school. The headmistress had objected to him speaking to the girls while tending the flower beds. Dan was upset by her seeming to place him in an inferior position (he had a university degree himself), so he went home and donned his batman suit, confronting the headmistress by saying that now he was

Batman, there was no way she had power over him. She was un-impressed with his argument and sent for the police. Dan was arrested as he reacted to the police dragging him off the property.

Since he was about to appear before the magistrate in this outfit, I felt sure (and probably rightly so), that the magistrate would think he was fit for a mental institute wearing such garb, and sentence him to hospital care. I persuaded the young man, after much argument, to change into an ordinary suit of clothes which were got for him to wear in Court. Dan never really forgave me for that action. He felt I had forced him into something he wasn't. He had wanted to present his argument to the magistrate as Batman and show that he could have power also in his own right. He resented the fact that I had persuaded him to act against what he believed in, and was not grateful to get off with a small fine.

Working with those in need has made me acutely aware of my own limitations in both my life and perceptions. I have been forced to see beyond the surface, and realise that each of us has a perspective on things that can be valid. It also has taught me to appreciate the specialness of each individual and the capacity for good and achievement in every human being. It is an approach that helps to bring out the good in us, and enables us to respond to life with optimism.

This is not to ignore the weaknesses in human beings or the collective malices and intolerances that exist. What often happens, however, is that our concentration on the things in others that are different or outside our experience leads us to reject them or rubbish them. The result is that we label people we don't like or who challenge us to change, and individually regard them as deviant, because they are different. There is no such thing as real normality or a 'normal' person. One Father's Day Dan presented me with a poem, 'To Father Felix':

I struggled through the sickly mud,
my journey shrouded in black blood.
For though the sun was shining bright
It was obscured by its own light.

Over my shoulders hung the moon
dull grey she was, like some aged tomb.
Hanging suspended upside down,
she sneered at me, her circus clown.
Oh la lune, la lune
Are you the romantic that we all swoon?

I want to dance a sunny song
but still you are there hanging on.
My way before me, clear as day
you are behind me leading the way.
Oh la lune, la lune
I don't want to dance to your luney tune.

Sizzling explosion, eggfried insane,
mental corrosion, egg scrambled brain.
Love, warmth and hope drained like the tide.
Fear washed over me, I was waiting to die
as blood dripped from the black gaps in the sky.
Oh la lune, la lune
won't you free me and the sea.

While my cranium creaks beneath the duel
I wonder if death is really that cruel.
For death ends pain, but for me god gives
a lifeless brain though my body lives.
Oh la lune, la lune
I'm afraid when you maim you don't look the same.

What are those white coats without eyes
That electric machine, sweet surprise?
Spastic scalp electrocuted brain
needles and pills for those not quite sane.
Oh la lune, la lune
do you cry 'more' as they bolt my door?

A golden girl with sunlight hair
suddenly showed me my career.
I howled at the pale moon that night
she was so weak, I screamed delight.
Oh la lune, la lune
I can't hear your crazy tune.

Derelict space ships pierce your side
behind a pimple complexion you hide.
A mere reflection of my Sun's rays
how did you get me in such a daze?
Oh la lune, la lune
is it much fun being eclipsed by the sun?

Though I still struggle through the mire
no longer is my soul on fire.
Today the sun is shining bright
guided am I by its clear light.

Over my shoulder hangs the moon
soft rays whisper a sweet love tune.
Candles, music, champagne on ice
Friends Sun and Moon, our Paradise.

On the top of the poem Dan had written a compliment ending 'You are my "Golden Girl" you might say; anyway happy Father's Day!'

I read this poem at Dan's funeral a few years later, when he hanged himself the day after Christmas from a tree in the Auckland Domain, close to my office, which was then in the pink cottage in the grounds of the Auckland Medical School. It was hard to read that poem — it was incredibly hard to bury Dan. Two friends who had helped Dan and lived with him during his time with us, Paul and Paula, were at the funeral. Paul was a young doctor who had helped me run the House while doing his medical training. The remarkable testimony to Dan was that it was the morning of their wedding.

The sad cross for me to bear was that Dan had rung Radio Pacific on his last night asking for me, but was told that I was not on air that night, though alternative help was available if he rang some other number. He never did. After the funeral his mother gave me Dan's Batman suit to dispose of as I would. At the funeral I also told the mourners that at the time of the disastrous fire that destroyed the Lloyd Avenue home, the most precious note of sympathy and help came from Dan. A scrap of pink paper accompanied a cheque for $100 with the comment: 'Lunatic asylums don't have much to offer (except insanity), but at Lloyd Ave I was treated as a human being — a nice change from the mental hospital. Thank you Felix. Lloyd Avenue can never be replaced, but I am sure another place will come up which is just as good. Love Daniel'.

It is not easy to determine what intervention or series of them effect changes in young people's lives. Sometimes it appears that new directions occur as a result of a friendship an alienated youth strikes up with an adult; or the discipline of a structured life, where previously there had been no order; or it could be a sense of personal affirmation a youth receives that brings a halt to previous unacceptable behaviour.

There are occasions when even the combination of all these factors appear ineffectual, at least at the time. In my memory Martin was such a person. He came to The Glade as a fourteen-year-old under the care of the Social Welfare Department. Various foster home placements had broken down and Martin had shown that he could not manage living in other people's families. He usually acted outrageously after an initial honeymoon settling-in period, and would then be rejected. Martin seemed almost to enjoy breaking up relationships that had begun very promisingly.

There were good reasons for his doing this. Martin lost his mother when he was four. The press reports over several days described how the remains of this woman in her late twenties were recovered scattered along a popular beach. Nine policemen found them, about five weeks after she had disappeared from her home. She was pregnant at the time. The coroner returned a verdict of suicide by drowning; Martin was not sure it was suicide.

Shortly after this the boy was placed in an orphanage, where he remained for five years. Then his father took him to England, but after a year put him on the plane back to New Zealand, stating he was out of control. Martin said he was left to his own devices a great deal and so got into mischief, including thieving and some prostitution. Martin's father had a number of wives and relationships over the years, and the boy felt excluded from these.

On his return to New Zealand, Martin was put into care and the series of foster homes started. He grew into an intelligent and good-looking youth. He was very self-willed and did not respond to discipline. He showed a pattern of stealing from those who were especially good to him or offered him affection. Little remorse or evidence of any conscience over what he did to people ever manifested itself.

The fact that he had no close family unit to belong to showed; he always wanted to be part of such a group. Some progress began to be made after he received closer parenting within The Glade, and left school. I wrote Martin a letter, outlining the perspective I had of him. I asked him to think my letter over, and see what was possible and what was not. First, I summed up all the positive things I had found in him, such as his quick intelligence, his friendliness, and the loving things he did, such as leaving little appreciative notes when something special was done for him. Then I went through the things that made it difficult to be close to him, such as his smart answers, his fear of showing his real feelings, his apparent lack of realising or caring how his behaviour hurt those who really loved him, and his dislike of anyone giving him directions. He often seemed to be acting a part, and the real Martin was hard to find.

I suggested some ideas for change — going on an Outward Bound course, joining a swimming club, saving up for a car, going with me to Vocational Guidance to check out job possibilities, working his way back up to his previous senior position in the House, and so on. I ended with a statement of caring for Martin, hoping that he would be able to talk about serious things with me, without feeling negative or closed off from me. I invited him to put in writing those things he expected from me or found difficult in relating to me as a father figure, as I said I wished to behave the way a real parent should.

This started off a good period in his life: communication improved, as did Martin's attitude and behaviour. He went with me to do a job suitability profile and from there got a position working with cars — the love of his life. Then things changed: he learnt that after all these years, his father was about to return to New Zealand with a new young bride. From then on he seemed to revert to his old behaviour and the influence I felt I had over him waned. He became aggressive and stubborn, and began to slacken off at his job.

At one stage he had expressed a keen desire to discover his mother's grave, so I eventually hunted down her burial place. But it was too late; he said he was no longer interested. When he had been making good progress, I had helped him buy a car; but as his behaviour worsened, so did his care of the vehicle, and he stopped bothering to pay it off. Eventually it was repossessed. Then Martin stole my car and burgled my flat. The car was eventually recovered, damaged, hundreds of miles from Auckland.

I tried to help him by getting him out of the city on to a farm. He bought a dog and seemed settled; but that ended after his father's arrival back in town. He was eventually sacked, and later returned to steal from his former employer. At length his crimes caught up with him and Martin was sentenced to corrective training in a penal institution. It was a heavy day for me when that happened — not that I disagreed with the sentence, but I couldn't help reflecting on the enormous amount of effort and care that had been put into Martin from many sources, only for this to be the result.

I often wondered what any of us could have done that would have brought about a better outcome for Martin. He was to tell me later that for him it was inevitable. He had never been able to cope with his mother's death and the belief that his father had murdered her. The rejection of him by his father in his youth left very deep hurts. He recalled the nightmares as a five-year-old in the orphanage. Afraid to sleep, he would try to stay awake as long as possible. The long lonely walk at night to the outside toilet was scary, and he imagined all sorts of shadowy people were out to get him.

Some nine months after Martin's release from Borstal, he wrote to me with affection calling me 'Dearest Felix', speaking appreciatively of what I had tried to do for him, and expressing confidence that he had learnt his lesson. So far so good. Now, several years later, Martin appears to be leading a settled and productive life. He has kept out of trouble and has a good relationship with a young woman. I would like to think that all the warmth and caring that went in over the years from social workers and foster parents had some impact, and cumulatively was of value in his reaching a level of maturity. Whether or not he would otherwise have been a hardened criminal is only a matter of speculation.

I marvel, given the horrendous experiences many youngsters go through, that they are not much worse than they are. If I had endured what some I have counselled have suffered, I doubt my own ability to survive. In spite of that, it is not always necessary for all seriously disturbed young people to sink to their lowest level before they are capable of change. Certainly there are some who seem to have to do so before there is any learning, but in my experience, that is not the case for most.

'My Life' was the heading on Joe's thoughts on the years up until he was fifteen.

I was borne Jan 8, and we lived in Ponsonby till I was 4 years old then we moved to Glen Innes and I went to the Glen Innes school when I was 5 and I did not like it I left when I was 14 and went to High School for 6 weeks then I got kicked out so I went and looked for a job and I could not get one and I needed some money so I done a job on a shop and got caught but I got let off that so I went and done some more and got caught again so I went to oy (Owairaka) and stayed there for 7 weeks and I went to the Glade and went to the Glade School for about 3 months then I stayed home for new years eve and came back to the streets and from there I got into more and more trouble. I done more jobs and I could not stop sniffing and I went back to the Glade and I got more and more home sick and so Warren let me go home a we bite more and I stayed doing want I always did giving my mother and father a hard time and I stayed sniffing again I want to learn to read and right and get a job and I will be good pleace let me come back I will be good Joe.

Joe was pleading to return to the Glade after running away and getting into trouble. His parents did not know how to control him; they were very concerned about their son, but he had a knack of making them feel guilty. As a result he had been able to con his mother into always getting him out of trouble and siding against her husband when he wanted to take a firmer line with Joe. Their son had an immense inferiority complex, especially regarding his small size. He tried to compensate by a bravado attitude and was easily led by his peers, since he constantly sought their friendship, no matter what the cost.

He was always promising to change his ways and improve his behaviour, but lacked the resolve to stay with such decisions. When he was in trouble with the law he would see his mother's great distress and show a great deal of remorse. It was one of those situations where the mother had a need to overcompensate her son by indulging his whims and being open to blackmail from him. Intellectually, she knew she had to be firmer with him, but was unable to put this into practice. Her resolve in that direction weakened, as did her son's in his particular behaviour.

Joe desperately needed to know from his mother and father that they loved him sufficiently to make him face limitations and to be accountable for his actions. He acted out constantly because he never received this direction from them. His usual state was one of depression; his criminal flings brought only more worry and remorse into his life. He hated and often spoke about the weakness he perceived within himself.

Ken differed from Joe in that he had no mother and yearned for one. I first met him when I picked him up outside Greenlane Hospital. He was due to move into one of our Houses and had lost his way getting there. At that stage he was eleven years old. He was a sad little boy; his body, as is often the case with emotionally deprived children, was short and undeveloped. There was almost a surliness toward me when I picked him up. It was clear he was not relishing the thought of moving on to yet another home.

Many a night I was to find him curled up on his bed clutching a photograph of his dead mother. Often he would have been crying. When he was a youngster, Ken had grown up seeing his parents making up packets of dope for distribution to the strange men who came to the house. Then his father had left for the Islands and Ken grew closer to his mother, though resenting the absence of his dad. When he was ten years old, his mother became ill, and Ken was suddenly whisked away to the country when she was admitted to hospital. For the next six months Ken pined for his mother and older sister, and to be back in Auckland to visit her. Those taking care of him said she was too ill to see him yet, and needed to be left on her own.

The news of her death was horrific for the boy and he felt lost and distraught. Unfortunately he had not seen her during the months of her dying from cancer, and so was unable to cope with her death. He was eventually brought back to Auckland and was fostered unsuccessfully in a number of homes. One of his constant pleas was to be adopted, and he asked this of one or two of the staff, including myself. I took him out one night to Radio Pacific, where I broadcast each Sunday evening. He enjoyed seeing a radio station in operation. At the end of the evening he handed me an envelope with the station's identification on it. Inside was a note with drawings — 'To Felix Thanks for taking me to your radio station, New Pacific. Love Ken your new son.'

Ken found it difficult to settle and kept hoping that his father would want him back. But he had made a new home and life for himself in the Islands, and did not want Ken intruding on his new family. He used to kid him along when he would call by phone. Eventually I wrote to him asking that he be honest with Ken and tell him his real intentions. The day his letter arrived, informing his son that there was no place for him in his home, we all knew what had happened. The boy was to be heard smashing things up in his room. When I got to him, he had ripped up anything that reminded him of his family. Photos, cards and letters all were destroyed in his anger at being rejected.

Later he searched to find where his mother was buried. We went through the records of various cemeteries, but no trace of her was to be found. Finally a relation told Ken that she had the ashes in her care. So we arranged, at his request, to have a burial service for his mother. Early one morning we went to the cemetery. Ken held the ashes in a small box. The tears fell down his cheeks as he placed it in the ground. I invited him to say something, but he shook his head. Then I suggested that maybe he would like to read something from the book I had, but he admitted to being unable to read it. So it ended with him saying some suitable words after me.

It was all over by 8.45 a.m., so I offered to drive the young boy back to school. He said he could not handle it. I suggested taking him back to The Glade, but he did not want any of the other residents to see him so distressed. So he ended up spending time with me. That event was quite a turning point in helping settle Ken, though he still goes from day to day feeling alone and very much without ties. Several times he has taken off to join his father overseas, but it has always ended in disaster.

It is understandable why a person like Ken feels rather anti-social and has acquired few skills in relating to others. He feels fate has deprived him of his heritage and a degree of resentment lingers on that has proved difficult to heal. To say that he has improved greatly over the years is not to deny the residue of hurt and bitterness that shows little sign of fading. Workers in residential care can do their best to ease the loss, but the wounds go deep. Time and ongoing support through everything, including rebellious outbreaks, are necessary for eventual healing.

PART TWO

The Youthlink Programme

(3)
The Crisis Centre

There are seven distinct parts to the operation of the Youthlink Trust. At the heart is the Crisis Centre. This provides a point of initial contact for anyone wishing to make contact with the project. It operates from rooms in a central Symonds Street building owned by the Auckland Hospital Board; the staff includes a family therapist and two social workers — one a Maori with skills in the language and culture of her people, the other trained in counselling and residential youth care. A psychiatric nurse, provided by the Hospital Board, is rostered with the team. A young trainee youth worker is also employed by the Centre. It is open five days a week, but many counselling sessions take place in the evening. An answering service directs after-hours calls to The Glade.

The service is free to the community and is used by people in various parts of Greater Auckland, as well as from other parts of New Zealand. The Centre acts as a filter for the Trust's residential Homes, conducting initial interviews, and placing appropriate candidates in one or other of the Homes or at times in other similar houses in the community.

The Crisis Centre offers rapid and effective support for any young person or family in need. It provides a careful listening and non-blaming approach to those seeking help, as well as providing alternatives for those who are feeling trapped. It also helps people sort out relationship problems, and personal or accommodation difficulties. Contact and help by phone or visit or both are offered. The endeavour is to bring together the resources needed to help people resolve their immediate problems. Where it is helpful, brief supportive family therapy is provided at the Centre in rooms designed for this purpose.

The service offered to the community comes in a variety of ways, including the giving of information, often about the resources available to the caller in the community. The Centre is careful not to duplicate the work of other agencies. Once a crisis is dealt with, however, the staff will often provide short-term therapy for those in need of this, rather than referring those in need of help to yet another source, where they would have to repeat a great deal of material.

Sometimes an emergency placement is made, while the staff helps assess long-term needs and makes plans for the young person's future. These placements are usually only for a few days at most, while more permanent accommodation is investigated or a return home arranged. All Department of Social Welfare referrals through the Centre are made in conjunction with the liaison officer appointed to the Trust by the Department.

Since it is a centre for meeting a variety of community needs, the demand is documented and collected for passing on to suitable authorities for consideration, so that necessary social changes can occur. Users of the Centre are followed up when possible, in order to check whether the help offered has proved effective, and whether any further assistance is needed. This also provides an evaluation of the Centre's work and whether it is meeting users' needs. The results of these follow-ups form part of the annual report the Centre prepares.

One important role played by the Centre is that of providing support for the staff and residents of the Youthlink Homes. Given the collective expertise of the staff, help can be offered through counselling, staff training, involvement in programmes within the Houses, and practical support for staff working in the residential care setting.

One of the early tasks of the Centre's staff was to work out a philosophy of operation that would be the basis for the interventions undertaken. It is worthwhile noting these, as they outline the approach to the young in need and their families. Regarding adolescence as a stage of development, the Centre believes that it is a time of transition and change for both an adolescent and his or her family. These changes are both internal and external, in that the young person is experiencing new needs and situations, and these should be addressed in positive ways by others, including the family. Socially, a young person's roles can alter, and closer associations often occur with those outside the immediate family. Independence and efforts toward separation from the closeness of family are features of growth. Adolescence can also be a time of crisis, as a person moves toward an adult identity, sorting out those values that are personal as well as part of the family identity. This period of development is one for experimentation, challenge, creativity and fun.

The Centre staff are aware that our society does not make a good job of preparing adolescents or their families well for these changes. The expectation seems to be for a sudden, uncomplicated move into adulthood. There is scant tolerance for any transitional period, and there are no clear rites of passage involved. Most youth problems are the result of a lack of recognition of legitimate needs, and of not making allowances for moving through what should be normal transitions. Moves toward being independent are often seen as rebellious or as an attack on authority, because of a lack of communication or a fear in the young person that his or her identity is being threatened or stultified. The resultant behaviour becomes a 'problem', though it can be simply an exaggerated attempt to become free or be their own person.

So-called 'deviant' or 'problem' behaviour can be seen as young people's solutions to the dilemmas they are in. While they work through these feelings and situations, they need time and space to themselves, until they feel ready to make choices. They are also in need of permission to make mistakes, without being constantly reminded of these. In other words, their mistakes should be seen as learning experiences, rather than as failures.

A strong article of faith for staff is that young people who face a society and future different from those their parents faced often express a sense of hoplessness, if not cynicism, about the world and their place in it. On their part, parents often feel distant from their son or daughter, and unable to be of help. In addition there are many pressures homing in on the family that are dislocating to family life. These could be anything from hair styles to cannabis smoking. The electronic media pressures young people to perform, sexually and emotionally, beyond their capabilities.

Youth tend to be very vocal about what is going wrong with society, and then feel they are held to blame as they listen to the constant put down statements beginning, 'Young people today...' They can easily believe they are being rejected, and so feel alienated from most of society as well as from their parents. Logic does not necessarily play a big part in such conclusions.

Given these factors, the Centre, in its dealings with the young and their families, tries to see adolescent problems in the context in which they originate and are experienced, namely family, culture and society. All resolutions attempted must take account of these. Respect has to be shown for the young and their families in any assistance offered, and also recognition that the adolescent is capable of making choices and decisions, then taking responsibility for those choices. The provision of adequate supports and resources to youth and family are important in this process.

While the young are encouraged to make choices, and the implications are discussed with them, they need affirmation of the decisions they make. For them, there must be a sense of having freedom to choose, rather than being forced to do what others think is right for them. This requires guidance rather than control from those working in this context.

Those working with teenagers must appreciate that they are capable of being caring and helpful. They also can come up with fresh ideas and are often resourceful and energetic. Underlying all these approaches must be youth's experience of being valued in their own right and not as some possession, such as somebody's child. In other words, it means relating to them as individuals and offering them, from an adult base, appropriate models to whom they can relate.

Crisis Centre workers believe that there are a number of major needs all adolescents have, including a sense of belonging and security. Closely interrelated is a belief in their self-worth. If they are to mature, they must know that they are able to have self-determination in major issues affecting their lives and future. It should be stressed that they want independence, respect, the experience of being listened to and accepted. They clearly seek responsibility plus accountability. They need to know they are loved sufficiently, that their parents will at times spell out the limits and say no. They also want reasons for the 'nos', and they can cope when there is consistency in adults' behaviour toward them.

Young people can have a surprising degree of insight into their own situation and weaknesses. Anyone working with them in a crisis situation needs to listen very carefully to these understandings they have. They want help to come to terms with their sexual identity, and be able to appreciate the range of choices that are theirs. They also seek approval from their peers, and are influenced by them. At times they will experience conflict between peer group expectations and what their parents expect, or in trying to conform to others' expectations.

When individuals come for help, the approach of the staff is to empower its clients to take charge of their own lives. This means assisting people to help themselves. So we work alongside people in a facilitating manner; this means that we try to generate a caring environment in which confidentiality is ensured and trust is able to develop. Staff try to provide choices for the users, suggesting alternatives, and facilitating the use of other resources.

No one is excluded from the Centre on grounds of race, sex, class, religion or education. It has a particular commitment to those who are disadvantaged or at high risk. Since it is a Crisis Centre, the immediate concerns have to be addressed first, and basic needs met, such as placement in a safe environment, adequate housing, clothing, nutrition, and a commitment to helping those in need. All this is to help people take charge of their own health and well-being.

The Centre operates as follows: each day a staff member is rostered on as responsible for all referrals or requests for help on

Operation of Crisis Assessment Centre

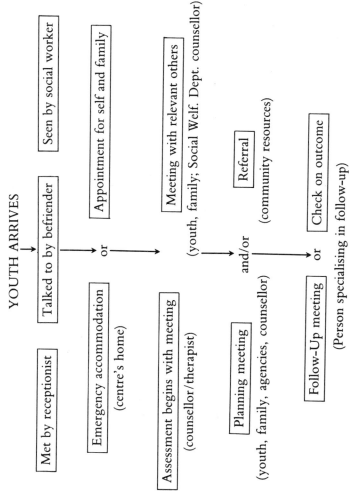

YOUTH ARRIVES

Met by receptionist

Talked to by befriender → or →

Seen by social worker

Emergency accommodation
(centre's home)

Appointment for self and family

Assessment begins with meeting
(counsellor/therapist)

Meeting with relevant others
(youth, family; Social Welf. Dept. counsellor)

→ and/or →

Planning meeting
(youth, family, agencies, counsellor)

Referral
(community resources)

→ or →

Follow-Up meeting
(Person specialising in follow-up)

Check on outcome

that particular day. The on-call person assigned for that day is there to provide back-up support and make decisions. All information is recorded in a referral book. This includes requests for information, or an appointment, or the need for advice and counselling which have been dealt with over the phone. The on-call staff member makes the decision as to whether or not the individual needs to be seen that day or whether a later appointment will do.

At the start of each working day, all referrals from the previous day which require action are assigned to the Crisis staff. The administrator is responsible for assigning referrals. The on-call staff member is responsible each day to ensure all referrals from the previous day have been dealt with as outlined. Name, address, phone number, staff member to whom assigned and referral number are then recorded in the Master List.

The person on the phone answers calls with an identification of the service and their own name. They find out whether the caller is the client, or what their relationship to the identified client is, their involvement with the problem, and their name, phone number and address. Then a description of the problem is asked for, noting details of the client's living situation, and whether there are others outside the family or living situation who are involved; who is legally responsible; and whether any other agencies or professionals are involved. It is also helpful to check whether the problem has been longstanding or short-term, any solutions already attempted, and the nature of the assistance now being sought.

The youth or person calling may be reluctant to give out much information. Staff are expected to respect this, while tactfully reminding the caller that more help can be offered if more is known. Confidentiality and the willingness to be available at any time are stressed. If the client wishes to be seen immediately, then this is arranged. Otherwise times suitable to the client are suggested for an appointment. Sometimes a more suitable resource can be suggested, but the client's choice is respected.

Regular staff meetings, training sessions, and a review of the work being done help keep the Centre on its toes and aware of community needs. When the Centre first started, it was thought that most use would be made of it by 'street kids', but though a number *have* taken advantage of its services, they are not highly represented among the referrals. It has been suggested that the problem about 'street kids' is not so much that they have no homes (many do have a home to go to), but that people do not like youngsters living on the streets. They seek help where and how they want it and are very distrustful of any agencies 'out to help them'. The Crisis Centre staff has tried to make its rooms attractive and to welcome young people with coffee and a warm reception when they call.

Though each sex is generally cared for by staff of the same sex, this is not an inflexible procedure. Once a week there is a full business meeting attended by the Director. Plans are promoted at this gathering, and new ventures discussed.

One factor has become clear: that it is often not the young person who is 'in crisis', but the teacher or social worker or referring parent. This does not mean the crisis is invalid, but it has a bearing on how the case is managed. So the emphasis in crisis intervention work is to identify the immediate problem, and to set a short-term goal for dealing with that problem, so that the person in crisis has their needs met. It is important not to plan further at that point.

The Centre staff are expected to believe all that the client tells them, only later checking out any discrepancies that may surface. The staff member becomes an advocate for the client as appropriate. Once the immediate crisis has been relieved, it then becomes possible to help those involved to look at causative and other important factors that are disturbing in their life, if they so wish.

After two years in existence, the Centre set itself some goals for the future. These include more reliable data collection for purposes of future funding, and to file information so that improvements can be made. Staff have also increased their outreach work into the community to meet individuals and groups, in order to stay in touch with current youth needs, to publicise the Centre, and to refine the work at Youthlink.

Since the Crisis Centre is only two years old at the time of writing, it is a little early to evaluate the service fully, or provide a clear picture of adolescent needs and the difficulties families are experiencing. Among the issues that have emerged is the problem of control. There often seems to be a struggle between a parent, more frequently a solo one, and the young person, over the direction he or she should be taking. In many cases the young person is inappropriately in control and the parent does not know how to change that, feeling inadequate and unable to cope.

The following is an analysis of the figures for the first year of operation. It needs to be kept in mind that for nearly half that time, the Centre was in rather inaccessible and difficult quarters (at the psychiatric hospital). The data covers 694 separate cases, including adolescents, families, and the combination of both.

The age range of young people seen at the Centre was from eight to twenty. However, only 1 percent were under twelve, while the largest groups interviewed were fourteen or fifteen years old. The next largest groups using the Centre were those aged sixteen and seventeen. Overall, 54 percent were males, and 46 percent females. The racial grouping was 73 percent Caucasian, 21 percent Maori and 6 percent Pacific Islander. The census data for the Auckland region (1981) shows that over 80 percent were Caucasian, over 8 percent Maori, and 7 percent Pacific Islander.

In the planning stages, critics had estimated that there would be few self-referrals to the Centre, yet the figures showed that the highest single source of referrals were from the young people themselves, or their families (34 percent). Other referral sources, in descending order, were voluntary organisations, Hospital Boards, and Department of Social Welfare. These averaged around 13 percent each of the total referrals. Educational sources sent 10 percent, and the Justice Department slightly under 9 percent.

People used the Centre in various ways. Twenty percent used it for telephone counselling, which could include crisis management as well. Fewer calls involved the giving of information and advice, or referral to other resources. Close to 52 percent were seen at least once at the Crisis Centre, and over 20 percent were consultations with the referring agent responsible for the client. Those who had appointments at the Centre usually needed only one appointment (57 percent), but 25 percent had from three to seven separate counselling sessions. Often the person was put in touch with community resources that could provide ongoing support, where this was needed.

The nature of the problems presented are difficult to tabulate, since what seems to be the initial problem can, after questioning, become less important to the young person and the interviewer, as some other issue emerges. For example, a girl seeking accommodation may reveal an incestuous relationship with her father. The problem areas catalogued during the first year, with actual numbers in brackets, are as follows: behaviour, especially criminal, violent and disturbing to others (392), family disruptions (338), non-coping behaviours (373), legal concerns (172), accommodation needs (121), medical needs (47), occupational and employment difficulties (40), financial problems (16), and educational difficulties (15). There were 92 requests for residential care in the Youthlink Houses.

All these cases are followed up where possible at monthly, three-monthly and six-monthly intervals. Clearly no follow-up is possible to an anonymous phone call, nor is it necessary when the need was transient, such as names of youth hostels. Many of the users of the service tend to move from address to address, so further contact can become impossible at times. It becomes difficult to check out the effectiveness of interventions when a youth does not want any contact made with his or her home, or when mail or phone calls from the Centre would create difficulties for the client.

Besides caring for the daily crises that occur, the Centre fulfils a number of other functions. Its solvent abuse programme is known to Youth Aid (police) and schools. These young people are helped through individual counselling, therapeutic work with the family and, where useful, the involvement of the young person and his or her family in support group work once a week. This segment of Youthlink's work was set up at the request of the police who work with young people.

The staff at the Centre put a lot of time into community educational activities. They give lectures to nurses, social work students and workers, groups working with youth and interested agencies. Talks are also given to school groups and teachers, and Centre staff assist in the training of student nurses, social workers, and students doing degrees, who spend anything from a day to nine months observing and working at the Centre. Public relations is seen as important; this is promoted through visiting agencies and giving help with some of their difficulties.

The Trust has also helped other organisations setting up to work with youth. We have been members of various groups set up to develop the work of residential care for youth, such as Te Whakakaianga, comprising many houses for youth living in the Auckland metropolitan area. The co-ordination of such groups and the wider population of all those concerned with needy young people is not easy. One of the things I have realised, over many years in youth work, is the reluctance of many to share resources or to work in closely with each other. The result has been duplication and overlapping of services. It is understandable that people working in a difficult, unpopular and often unrewarding area of social need are so preoccupied with their own agency or home and its survival that they have little energy for sharing with others. It is easy to become myopic in such work, and even to fear outside scrutiny, and inevitably some criticism, so that working with others is a low priority.

While the Centre is ready and willing to provide support and share resources with those working in similar areas, this side of its work is not often taken up by others. I am presently chairman of the Adolescent Forum, an Auckland body concerned with advancing the quality of service to the young and promoting the growth of needed resources. Its members comprise people from Government agencies concerned with health, education and social needs, as well as those working in Youth Aid, adolescent psychiatric services, residential homes and voluntary workers involved with the young.

Through regular meetings and special seminars, youth workers come to appreciate what others are doing for the young and what needs are not being met within the community. We have held live-in weekends, one day gatherings and some regional support sessions concerned with issues of parenting, violence, solvent abuse, education, crime, alcohol abuse and youth rights. A feature of many of the sessions has been the co-operative sharing between Maori, Pacific Island and Pakeha adults working with young people. It was the Adolescent Forum which was instrumental in getting the Crisis Centre from planning stages to a reality, so we have a commitment to helping it help others.

(4)
Entering Residential Care

Joe knocked on my flat door at the Greys Avenue Home near midnight one summer evening. In one hand he held a knapsack, in the other a copy of my book *Candles in the Wind*. He had hitch-hiked from New Plymouth, and as a result of reading the section in that book on the House I ran, he had decided that this was the place for him. The sixteen-year-old was exhausted and hungry. It had taken two days to make it to Auckland. He was also frightened, and now had doubts about coming so far. He had confusion over his identity, including his sexuality, and felt despairing of being able to sort things out for himself. My book had given him some promise of help, and here he was. However, he had romanticised the Home; its size and numbers were already giving him second thoughts.

While the Houses are havens for many young people, they are also staffed and inhabited by ordinary people who have needs and tempers, moods and resentments. At times these can dominate and make the atmosphere difficult. Tension can be high. Joe had to learn to cope with these pressures as he came to terms with his problems. He enjoyed the times spent in the one-to-one relationship of counselling, but his shyness made the give-and-take of daily living with twenty-three others very demanding. It took some time for Joe to appreciate that the help he needed was not just tied up in therapy sessions, no matter how much he valued these, but that many of his difficulties would be worked through in the shared living with a community of young people. It is fine to meet this young man again now, to find him making a good life for himself, and to know that he has achieved fulfilment.

Today, everyone who wants to enter one of our Houses is screened at the Crisis Centre. Staff have a number of options to choose from. *The Glade* is for young people aged between ten and sixteen, and holds about thirty residents.

On the site of the Glade is the *Glade School*. It enables us to provide special teaching facilities for those residents who have not been able to cope with ordinary schooling, or who have special learning difficulties. Staffed by one full-time and several part-time teachers, it takes up to sixteen pupils in two divisions: an academic section, which follows more traditional subjects, and a creative, alternative programme. At times both groups combine for activities (e.g. Sports or Maori cultural programmes). The pupils' progress is reviewed from time to time to assess their readiness for outside schooling.

For older residents (from fifteen to twenty-five years) there are around thirty beds at *Rowan House* in Mt Roskill. While both The Glade and Rowan House take fifteen-year-olds, the policy is to place those at school or able to cope with classes at The Glade, while those out of work or finished with school go to Rowan House. From there we run a Work Preparation or Day Programme which takes in all those residents who are out of work or not on any programme occupying them during normal working or school hours. It takes place at a hall in the area and is run by a staff member with special skills in motivating young people and helping them find employment. There are usually about twenty on this programme. The Glade operates its own programme for those not at school or work.

The *Family House* at Rowan Road is a home for young children. It provides accomodation for those young residents who are likely to be with the Trust for a long time. The idea is to provide a smaller living experience (eight young people at most) for those who would benefit from the closer knit environment. The Mt Albert *Muriel Kerr-Taylor House* is for girls only, who may be at risk or have suffered abuse from males. Some move when ready into the larger mixed Homes. Several beds are kept open for emergency female referrals, while their needs are being assessed. All Administrators of residential Homes are women.

Each of these Homes is different in character and in style of operation. The Glade is a large, attractive two-storey building set in over two acres of bushland, bordered by the motorway. It was once the home of businessman Sir William Goodfellow, and his large concrete bomb shelter still stands at the entrance to the property. While the grounds are large, there is little playing area, hence the importance of the large recreational hall.

In recent times it has become evident that we need to have a small home for girls only. This is to provide a safe place for those young females who have been sexually abused and need time away from males to gain their security and work through their fears. This needs to be away from young males, who could take advantage of their vulnerability. The home is in its planning stages at present, and will be run by female staff. It is envisaged, that such residents will probably move into a mixed living situation in due course, when it is clear they are able to cope with such demands.

Rowan House has a commanding site, with spacious grounds. There are more single rooms here, than in any other of our other homes. The Muriel Kerr-Taylor House is much smaller, but it also has a large area of land in front of it. It is up a long driveway near the St Lukes shopping centre.

Depending on space available at the time of interview, the Crisis Centre staff suggest one of the Homes for a young person needing accommodation. Once contact has been made with all those involved, especially (for the younger resident) with the parents, then planning for admission can proceed. In order to get an involvement with the parent(s), we ask them to sign jointly with us a commitment to supporting their son or daughter in our work with that young person. This document covers the Trust's responsibilities as well as those of the parent(s). Any points of difficulty in it are talked over with the family, to ensure that they are happy with the contract and are prepared to keep it. They are advised that they are most welcome to get in touch with the staff at any time they have concerns.

The importance of this commitment is stressed with parents before the Trust becomes fully involved with the youngster. Willingness on the part of the parent(s) to work with us as far as they reasonably can is a prerequisite for admission. However, we will never turn a young person away if for any reason the parent(s) will not or cannot assist. But we push for that co-operation as a starting point, because so many youth problems centre around relationships with parents.

Before a final decision about entrance is made, the young person and those involved are invited to visit the particular Home that seems appropriate for residency. All being well, the individual then moves into the Home. A Special Person is assigned to the new resident, to welcome them on arrival and introduce them to various people. If that Special Person cannot attend the arrival, a substitute is arranged. They have seen that the bed and room are ready for the newcomer. A senior resident is also appointed to take a special interest in the new arrival during the first three weeks of residence.

In the Trust, we have grown to believe that it is essential to put a good deal of input into a young person immediately before and after they arrive. For this reason, we have developed a number of procedures which help to ensure that initial attention is provided. In times of staff shortage or overcrowding, it is easy to neglect these initiation programmes, and all are the losers as a result. A resident quickly learns how to work the system, if there are loopholes, and it is hard to regain the initial willingness to co-operate or the early reluctance to test the staff and programmes.

Normally, for the first week of settling in, the person does not attend school or work, but is absorbed into the Home. However, this luxury is not always possible, and we balance it against the need to go to work or keep up with school assignments or programmes. The resident is shown the Manual explaining what is required of those living in the Home. This covers material that would also have been explained during the meetings at the Crisis Centre.

After the resident has settled in, planning takes place to ensure that his or her needs are met. For the first three weeks, the resident is on what is called an assessment programme. This covers an observation of the person's daily behaviour, based on predetermined criteria, and is monitored by a staff member. There are seventeen items on which residents are graded on a 0 to 5 scale. The lowest level is 0, meaning a bad performance or few of the requirements adhered to. At the highest level of 5, the resident and staff know that all requirements were fulfilled in an excellent manner. A staff member (or, in Rowan House, a senior resident) will decide on the scoring with the resident each evening. In this way the young person is aware of his or her daily progress.

The items listed are: personal cleanliness; performance of house jobs; attendance at school, work or Day Programme; abstinence from alcohol or drugs; keeping set bedtimes; payment of weekly board (when applicable); care of the fabric of the House; attendance at House meetings; displaying a co-operative attitude toward staff; a positive and caring attitude toward other residents; attendance at any groups or study requirements; peaceful sharing of bedroom and tidiness in it; evidence of self-motivation and initiative; cleaning tasks outside (e.g. grounds or vans); staying on the property as required, and not leaving without permission; taking part in leisure activities and general mixing with other residents.

On the successful completion of these three weeks of close observation, the resident is told in front of the House staff and residents that he or she is now fully accepted as a resident and is at the starting level in the House. A special welcome is given and a commitment to the resident is given by management. The young person is now encouraged to move through the various levels toward the top one, which means the process of exiting (unless the youth needs to make his or her permanent home with us) is under way.

The process of evaluation continues, as outlined in Chapter 11. The staff member and resident work out the goals that are necessary for the young person to gain something worthwhile and measurable from living in the House and working through its programme. The goals, long- and short-term, are reviewed bi-monthly with the resident, and the grading made is a measure of progress or lack of it. These sheets are referred to in planning meetings and other discussions relating to the resident's progress.

The initial referral interview would have indicated what school or work programme should be followed. Now the individual is enrolled in the appropriate course. His or her consent is essential for this to succeed. A staff member, usually the Special Person for the resident, accompanies him or her to a school enrolment or a job interview.

Checks are made during the course of a residency as to whether the processes planned actually occur. The most important questions centre around the Special Personning; the key ones are, 'Is the resident being seen weekly by that staff member? What is the quality of the relationship?' Goal progress (particularly the steps toward making sure they are met) is checked by administrative staff. If there is no advancement being made, then the reasons for this are investigated and discussion takes place as to what additional resources might be needed.

Shaun was a sixteen-year-old who at times had most of the staff scared of his reactions when he was thwarted. He had threatened to kill or hit staff at various times. While he encountered the consequences, the uneasiness of the staff remained. He made some progress in his goals, such as getting permanent work and desisting from thieving; but all this was jeopardised by his seemingly ungovernable temper and deep-seated anger. In talking over this boy's problems with him at a senior staff level, we asked him what he thought was necessary.

Shaun admitted at times to completely losing control, and this frightened him. He recalled that there had been a time when he had taken to a teacher with a broom, and threatened another with a knife, so he had been placed on medication. During the two months that followed, Shaun said he had not had one violent episode. So we worked out that he would undergo regular intensive therapy with two Youthlink counsellors, and at the same time have medication to help while he worked toward his own independent control of his violence. These measures proved effective, and eventually broke the block to his attaining those goals important in his life, especially getting a girl friend who felt safe with him and who was not threatened by any violence on his part.

Part of the assessment that goes on after a young person comes into our care is to see how things are working out at the family level. Family therapy sessions are used to help movement all round, and to bring a deeper awareness of each others' needs to all

63

parties. They are not necessarily trying to get the young person back home as soon as possible. Staying with practical behavioural issues, such as school or work attendance, or positive measurable behaviours, enables those concerned to determine whether progress is being achieved, or whether more initiatives are needed.

The length of stay varies according to age, family support, motivation, the togetherness of the House the resident is in, and whether or not there is suitable alternative accommodation. We find the younger residents tend to stay about four months longer than the older ones. Some will clearly be with us till they are capable of living independently. The average length of stay at Rowan House is five months, and nine months at The Glade; but at any one time there are about ten residents who have no prospect of returning home, and who are likely to be with us for four or more years.

One of the facilities we have is the ability to move residents around within our own system. Given the number of Homes we have, we are able to move an individual whose stay is not working out at one Home, though it is not a totally new experience, since a fair amount of intermingling already occurs. While the different Homes are used for temporary suspensions of youths whose behaviour has become impossible where they are because of violence or abuse of staff, they can also be used for a permanent transfer.

Sometimes, when a youth has been suspended overnight or for several days, it can become clear to everyone that he or she would be better off in the new placement, because the age range is more suitable or a better rapport with staff is achieved. We are always sensitive to such rearrangements, and carefully talk them through with all concerned. Since the Homes have different degrees of freedom operating, some young people respond much better to a tighter regime, and others to more self-motivated responsibility.

If one administration believes a given resident should leave because of lack of progress, hassles with staff or residents, a bad reputation gained and so staying in a fixed role, or an imbalance of certain types of residents, then there are procedures for transfer. First the staff meet at the Home where the resident is living, to discuss whether the youth should move on, and if so, where. The Special Person involved is expected to be part of this decision-making.

Should the recommendation be to shift the resident to another Youthlink Home, consultation then takes place with the proposed new administration. If the move is accepted, this staff carry out an interview and the conditions of stay are negotiated. Usually a trial period is suggested to see how the change works out for all concerned.

While we try not to make rules 'on the run', we often find that new circumstances mean we have to reshape old procedures or invent new ones to fit changed circumstances. Staff, let alone residents, need clear guidelines and expectations in order to provide security and consistency for all. Following through all requirements takes a great deal of monitoring, but is essential for everyone's good.

Often, as I drive from one property of the Trust to another, I think back to the early days of Youthlink, when there was a minimum of structure and most of my project time was spent with the residents. Now my preoccupation is with staff, in particular the administrators of the various sections. I get slightly worried at the amount of structuring that has become necessary, as the age range has broadened and society itself become more stressed, generating increasingly complex behaviour problems among the young. While I try to keep rules and structures to a minimum, the dictates of accountability to agencies, neighbours, and different needs among the young have meant that basic systems have been set up and much of my energy has to go into seeing they are adhered to.

It has also become clear that many of the youngsters coming into care are in need of security, and that the type of structures I am about to describe have helped provide a sense of safety. One that has been functioning for the past five years is a tiered system. There is nothing original in the idea of residents in a programme starting at a lower level and earning the right to move progressively toward increased responsibility and independence.

When we moved to The Glade, we devised a four-stage transition process through the House. The concept centres around the fact that young people respond to the opportunity to gain recognition for effort by promotion to a new level involving more privileges and status within the system. With the residents of the time, we spent a day working out what the grades in the Home would be, and the attendant rights and responsibilities. The levels were named after the different properties that had formed part of our history. At the time of naming, we had lived in three houses, but as four levels were seen to be necessary, we divided one of the names into two levels.

Our first Home had been at Lloyd Avenue, so we called the initial group *Lloyds*. Then there were *Greys* (after the Greys Avenue Home), *Senior Greys* and *Almorahs* (The Glade is in Almorah Avenue). Later, when we established Rowan House at Mt Roskill, the top level there became *Rowans.*

What is required at each level varies from time to time, but this is the basis:

Lloyds: This is the lowest level. A resident is at this stage for at least three weeks. Evidence of stable behaviour is required before moving to the next stage. Youths in this grade do not have voting rights at House meetings, are not allowed to leave the property without permission, and have a lower pocket money grant. Lloyds also go to bed earlier than the others, and have less choice in what cleaning tasks they do. A resident moves out of this grade if there is attainment of sufficient points.

Greys: At this stage, in addition to the requirements for Lloyds, residents are expected to show a loyalty to those living and working in the House and an ability to take some initiatives in helping themselves and others. They are allowed to go to bed half an hour later than when they were Lloyds. They can leave the property on their own, whereas Lloyds had to be accompanied by a senior resident, but permission to leave is still required; and they receive more pocket money. Movement to the next level depends on the level of points reached.

Senior Greys: This level is really a preparation for becoming an Almorah or Rowan. It is a trial as well as a training period: it requires taking responsibility for seeing to the good order of the House, and maintaining consistency in working through individual goals. Senior Greys are expected to show steadiness in behaviour, including school, work or day programmes. Evidence of leadership qualities is looked for too, though this is not essential for promotion. Overall reliable and acceptable behaviour are required for progression to the top level. Recommendation for promotion comes from attaining a high number of points.

Almorahs or Rowans: The number at this level is usually no more than eight, and a high standard of consistent behaviour is required. To remain in this group, residents must meet the following criteria: they must show loyalty to the House, be respected by other residents, and set a consistent standard in keeping the major rules. They are basically stable in their lives, and are prepared to work co-operatively with staff in building up a good atmosphere and keeping good order. They maintain a tidy room, are not into violent behaviour, and show willingness to take a leadership role; their overall behaviour sets a standard for other residents. These behaviours are reflected in the points system, which is an objective assessment of these qualities.

The philosophy behind the tiered system in the Houses is to give young people motivation to work on changes in their lives, set measurable achievements, and provide goals that have meaning for them. The system provides residents with examples of what is acceptable behaviour, and gives them opportunities to take responsibility and exercise leadership skills. It also helps develop a sense of tradition in the Houses.

From what has already been said, it is clear that a resident would have to provide evidence, over a reasonable period, of consistency in the behaviours required for promotion. For the senior levels they must show they are not involved in drug or alcohol abuse, are maintaining a school or job programme, and are not involved in an intimate relationship with another resident. The levels are subject to review: residents are demoted for actions that are against the rules of the House, and are considered serious infringements; or if, over a period of time, a resident is not living up to the standards required at that level. Demotion from the top grade is considered a serious matter, and some weeks must elapse before reinstatement can be considered.

If an Almorah or Rowan commits a criminal offence or is involved in serious drug behaviour, he or she is demoted and has to work back up, with fresh contracts to keep. In such cases the issues are talked over in the first instance with the resident concerned, and then publicly discussed at a House meeting.

The emphasis in movement of residents is not on privileges, though these are important, but on personal self-esteem and the growth that comes from achieving progress and working through the requirements. Admittedly a Rowan or Almorah receives twice the pocket money given to a Lloyd, but it is frequently pointed out that there are more important bonuses from progression in the system. One of these is the experience of leadership and the responsibility given; these are invaluable, and the benefits carry into later life. Such character training long outlasts passing privileges. Another valued result of being in the senior levels is the experience of working closely with staff in management, decision-making and socialising.

When the tier system was introduced, it soon became evident that those at the top level needed a large amount of support and training. So it has always been insisted on that those in the Almorah or Rowan group attend weekly training and support sessions. These are usually run by two staff members, including an administrator. They also hold their own business meetings without a staff member present, where they bring up issues of concern and present them to staff for attention. For the effective running of the Houses, it is essential that good relations are fostered between staff (especially administrators) and senior residents.

In practice, the young people in the Houses set great store by the tier system, and it has been well worth the amount of energy expended on making it work. What has to be remembered by staff working with senior residents is that they are still young, they are still working out personal problems, and they do require appreciation for what they are doing. It is also necessary to remember that they have loyalties to their friends and peers, so these must be respected and confidentiality maintained.

It is also necessary to watch that too much responsibility is not placed on them, so that they end up misbehaving in order to cope. Sometimes it is good to allow them time out from being a senior resident, so that they do not have to take responsibility for a period. It is also understandable that they will have lapses in behaviour from time to time, as they are still in the process of taking control of their lives. As long as these are not serious slips, then they can be readily dealt with.

The behaviour management programme that operates in the two larger residential homes is out to acknowledge positive behaviours and to help the resident match his or her performance against standards that are basic to successful independent living. The residents are able to move towards higher privileged levels by demonstrating a standard of behaviour expected for each level. The frequency of undesirable actions is decreased by consistency in disciplinary actions.

The programme operates under three headings — house routines, discipline areas and set behaviours targeted for the resident to achieve. Each of the categories are allocated a preset number of points each shift. The residents earn these points for the specified desired behaviours or they are fined preallocated points for various undesirable behaviours.

The house routines provide incentives for each resident to comply with the daily structure of the house and to meet staff requests. The points operate on an 'all or none' basis, which means points are only earned, if a task is completed to the level described in the definition of the task. The level for each resident in the status scheme (Lloyds, Greys, Senior Greys and Almorahs or Rowans) is set by the number of points necessary to stay at that level or move higher.

The house routine covers bedroom care and behaviour, functioning at meals, personal hygiene, performance of house cleaning tasks, and activities undertaken as prescribed during the day. These include attendance and performance at school, work preparation programme, employment programmes or work.

The discipline category covers a range of three types of maladaptive behaviours, that are graded according to their level of seriousness, with criminal and drug activities at the higher grade down to the breaking of house rules. Besides losing points in the system for such behaviours, a resident can have privileges withdrawn, written contracts required, grounding to the house, suspension, referral to the police or apologies to anyone affronted.

All residents have the right of appeal against what they consider unfair or excessive punishment or victimisation, or if they feel they are innocent. The resident must first comply with the directive given. After completion of the set consequences, the resident may go to the resident representative or a staff member and state their case. A group, including a resident, will look at such complaints.

The target behaviours are specific desirable actions or problem areas suited to a given resident. These behaviours are worked out with the resident and Special Person each week, and have specific tasks set for each day. These are assessed at the end of each shift and points awarded for attempts at the tasks, while full points are given for the completion of the task. These points can be interchangeable for privileges or against discipline points.

There is a related area called personal achievement, which recognises positive behaviours a resident may demonstrate during a period of observation, which would usually be during the evening shift.

All these points are totalled and the subject of weekly publication at house meetings, with recognition provided for achievements. Those who are not making progress or whose behaviour has placed them at the lowest level, meet with the Director and Administrator of the House after the meeting, to look at what is happening for the resident. The object of this assessment programme is to make it as objective a measure as possible and to provide the young people with an accurate measure of their behaviour over the past week.

The standards of evaluation remain constant and do not rise or fall according to residents' performances. The standards that are required are those that are seen as reasonable in society in general, and are therefore a good preparation for meeting these social requirements on leaving the Trust's care.

This approach means that we concentrate on positive rather than negative behaviour, which happens if you do not have some clear structures. Punitive measures in this approach become secondary, as the need to apply them decreases within this system. Residents are anxious to score well, so as to gain or maintain a position of status within the House. It also diminishes the number of staff-resident conflicts, as the programme exists independently of the given staff member.

The system takes some effort from staff to make it work, and they have to be consistent. There is a fair amount of paperwork involved, but the results are worth it. Besides providing feedback to the residents, the numerical scores are also an indication of progress or lack of it, and any dramatic changes in behaviour are clearly indicated. This information can be of great value to administrators and counsellors; a drop in scoring suggests the surfacing of emotional problems that require immediate attention. Scores also provide material for the Special Person-President interaction.

For at least half of Youthlink's history, there was a heavy emphasis on counselling as a major factor in our work with the young. It is still there, but is now strongly balanced with other things such as exercise, diet, and development of personal skills. As the project grew, we called in more volunteers to assist with counselling of residents. These trained people were allotted a given number of residents whom they saw weekly. What we came to appreciate over time was that we were in danger of creating sick or misbehaving roles, so that residents could feel they had worthwhile things to discuss in the counselling session! It also tended to develop an introspective approach for some residents; others became jealous when they heard of some sophisticated technique used by another resident's counsellor. After some discussion with our Psychiatric Consultant at the time, Dr Muriel Taylor, we changed to a concept of providing each resident with what we called their Special Person. The aim was to move away from a counselling relationship with a staff member to that of a type of parent-friend encounter. This development has proved successful, and has been in operation now for four years.

The objectives of Special Personning are to help a resident feel at home and cared for in a living situation with a large number of

70

people. It is a guarantee that each resident has an adult on the staff who takes a personal interest in them and is there for them to share whatever bothers them. Young people have a say in who will be the staff member allotted to them; but occasionally their first choice might be a person already heavily committed, and so someone else has to be selected.

Our intention in this scheme is to provide the following supports for each resident:

- An *advocate* within the system, so that their case is always fully and carefully considered from their perspective, as well as others.
- An adult who will act in the role of a *parent-type* figure to the resident, attending to his or her personal hygiene, clothing needs, appearance and general good health.
- A person who will ensure the *evaluation* file is up-to-date.
- An adult who will spend *quality time* with a resident, in a relaxed and regular manner.
- A staff member who maintains contact with any parent(s), and others interested.
- A person who makes known any special needs or problems a resident is having, and keeps administrators informed of such matters.
- A person who notifies others of any special difficulties a youth is going through, and gains support for them.
- The Special Person attends training and supervision sessions so as to be able to offer as much skilled help as possible.
- This person also attends all meetings relating to the well-being of and planning for a resident.

It is vital that the Special Person does spend time with each allotted resident, and works on the relationship. Problems arise if a young person is not regularly seen, and acting-out behaviours can result. Sometimes a resident wants a change of person because he or she feels unheard by the staff member, senses some dislike, or has a communication block with that individual. There are also occasions when a young person dislikes the insights a staff person has and does not want to face up to the mirror-image that is being presented.

A real difficulty with the system is when staff in this special role leave. Residents can become very attached to staff, and feel let down when this movement out of their life occurs. We try to make the transition as painless as possible, and provide for a period of separation to occur prior to the staff leaving. We also ensure that a replacement is introduced to the young person, so that they do not feel neglected or alone. Some Special Persons have counselling skills and are able to meet most of their assignee's needs in that area. Others, recognising their limitations, request some extra counselling from another staff member for their resident, and this is readily arranged.

While Special Personning is a key factor in our programme of care, it does not mean that the only staff who become close to a resident are those assigned to that role. We find that residents use the staff in different ways to meet their needs. Sometimes they share concerns with an administrator, or other staff, which they do not wish to speak of with their Special Person. This happens in families, where children at different times confide in their mother or father something that they do not wish to tell the other parent. They usually want their Special Person told.

Of all the work that supervisory staff do, this is the area they find most satisfying, and they feel it often makes the other stresses of the job bearable. Youngsters who feel abandoned or rejected are slow to trust adults, but when they do can become extremely close, and in some ways dependent. They will share secrets they have carried all their lives. Some of these are deep hurts or shames that they are ultimately glad to unload. Confidentiality is respected in this situation, and Special Persons are required to get their client's permission before revealing personal secrets to others. The conflict that can arise over factors of safety, reputation and so on are worked through carefully, so that damage is not done through such disclosures.

Not all staff are given the role of Special Person to residents. Those selected are expected to have special skills of relating and stability, so that neither they nor the young people are at risk. The supervision they receive, and the feedback from residents, gives a reasonable indication of how they are succeeding with their brief. Usually a Special Person would work with four to six residents, in general of the same sex. However, some young people get on better with members of the opposite sex, sometimes because of unfortunate experiences with a parent or other significant person of the same sex. We are happy to accommodate individual needs, so that the right mix of personality and skill is achieved.

We have long felt the need for an exiting house, especially for our long-term residents. This could provide an opportunity to move from living with a large group into a smaller 'flat' type situation; this would enable them to learn cooking, budgeting and housekeeping skills which are difficult to teach in a large group situation. Up till now, we have not had the resources to set up such a scheme adequately. Successful exiting of many of our young people has been something of a weakness in our organisation, at least for the longer term residents, who can become rather dependent on us and lack skills to be self-reliant. In the past, youngsters who have been State Wards for many years have found it difficult to become self-sufficient. Part of our problem has been a shortage of staff who can spend time ensuring the exiting processes are thoroughly followed. The individual can make a hasty decision, the law might intervene, or behaviour can be so destructive that a resident has to leave in a hurry. In the heat of some of those situations it is not easy to arrange for tender, loving farewells.

We have learnt to try and plan exits from the Houses as far ahead as possible. This means that in discussions monitoring a resident's progress, we all need to bear in mind whether it is, or soon will be, time for the person concerned to be on their way. If, collectively, this is considered to be the right move, then the resident is consulted as to his or her feelings on the matter. Once it is established that the resident is now ready to move on, the Special Person works out with the youth the support systems that will be available once away from the Trust. Help in obtaining alternative accommodation and budgeting for the move are provided. Sometimes the youth feels ready, but has not saved enough for a deposit on a flat. The exiting might be delayed till sufficient funds are in hand to make the move possible. This can be a good incentive for saving money.

We try to work through the break from the House over a period, in which feelings about leaving, positive and negative, are resolved. Conditions of leaving are spelled out (e.g. notice to us, payment of debts and notification to any responsible agency). Together, the Special Person and the resident go over the time spent in the Home, stressing gains, goals achieved and contributions made, as well as friendships formed. Any pain at leaving should be worked through. Where possible the youngster is farewelled during an evening meal, with something special on the menu, to acknowledge their part in the life of our ongoing family.

The Special Person is asked to do a follow-up, and offer whatever support may still be needed. The youngster is not encouraged to keep hanging round the House on leaving, but to time visits back, so that dependency does not develop or continue. When someone is dismissed from the House or leaves without any preparation, residents discuss their feelings, including any sense of

73

loss or anger. Often the young person will make contact at a later date, and some delayed healing work can then take place. Sometimes, when they leave in this way, without completing the goals they were after, they will come back asking to be given another chance. Most times, they get it.

(5)
Changing Problem Behaviour

Over the fifteen years of running the homes for young people, it has become necessary to develop various ways of dealing with problem behaviours. Taking in a younger age group has meant that there have had to be more controls. As there has been evidence of increasing violence in society, with more assaults, rapes and verbal abuse, these reactions have shown in the young people coming into care. The racial tensions that are also part of this period of history manifest themselves in anger and frustration among the young.

Most of those coming for help have lacked appropriate controls in their lives. While they do want these from us, nevertheless they strain against the restrictions and test them to the limits. While we try to emphasise positive actions, and reward those, it is essential for the young to know there will be consequences for everything they do. The difficulty is to avoid responding only to negative acts, and taking all others for granted or ignoring them, so that the child learns that bad behaviour gets attention. Many a youth has told me that the reason for their misbehaviour is to gain attention from their parents. They can gain satisfaction from stealing a car, because it means their parents have to attend court, or visit them, or be interviewed by authority figures.

Over the years, rules have been established and worked through with the residents at various times. Usually half a day or more is spent with residents when major changes are made regarding rules. Sometimes this has taken place on camps lasting several days; at other times a Sunday morning is set aside for residents to give their views on behaviours that are causing considerable disruption to the good order of one or other of the Houses.

One of the noticeable differences in running residential homes now, compared with my first experience in 1962, is the increased violence one has to deal with. There were times in those early days when young people threatened to, or actually did, attack physically. But there is much more likelihood of that happening now than twenty years ago. Usually any physical damage I sustain is received in the course of trying to calm down a drunk or very disturbed youth after a staff member perhaps dealt somewhat insensitively (given the resident's condition) with the situation. Punches in the face or kicks in the groin are readily suffered in such circumstances.

Today, most of the problems arise when a resident has been drinking or smoking cannabis. Some of them become very aggressive and are extremely hard to manage. Unfortunately, underage youngsters find it very easy to get hold of alcohol, and all the rules in the world are of little avail. If the person has a recognised drink problem, rather than the occasional excessive use of alcohol, he or she is required to undergo therapy and be on a strict no-alcohol regime, as long as we keep them in our care. Otherwise staff and residents as well as property come in for a battering.

At times some residents can be extremely provocative and give staff a very hard time. They can goad, tease or insult a given staff member, trying to provoke their anger. Staff must have a great deal of self-control, and not be over-stressed, for them to cope with such provocations. A list of policies has been devised for the guidance of staff in these cases.

They are summed up in the Staff Manual. Briefly, they are as follows: No member of staff may physically hit or push a resident. If physical restraint of a resident becomes absolutely necessary to protect someone or to safeguard House property, it must be limited to the minimum for the purpose. Physical restraint is forbidden where non-co-operative behaviour is involved. Other strategies must be used.

Any of the following events must be recorded in a log book kept in each House: physical restraint of a resident; violence by a resident; violence by a staff member; any punishments of residents, noting date, nature of behaviour, and consequence meted out; any criminal behaviour, including action taken as a result; any involvement with the police. The Director or Deputy must be shown the book each week at the individual meetings with administrators.

So that this policy is adhered to, staff must ensure that their own stress levels are attended to, by taking reasonable breaks and seeking whatever support is necessary. The Director cannot support actions that are not reported as required, or where procedures are not followed. Any complaint by a resident or staff member regarding physical violence must be recorded, and the administrator of the House, as well as the Director, notified.

The problem lies in what 'other restraints' can be used that are effective and do not violate our policy. Some institutions have a 'time out' place where an out-of-control young person is placed until they have calmed down or are open to reason. This is usually a secure room that the youth cannot damage.

Some people oppose this practice, regarding it as primitive. There is another technique known as 'the Michael Whiting Holding' strategy. This involves one or two adults holding a boy or girl with his or her arms crossed in front of them and held by the adult, while they are restrained between the adult's knees. At times this holding can last for two hours or more. During this time, the adult does not speak with the child or youth. In my experience, this method of control has very positive effects. Above all, it produces a bonding of the difficult youngster to the adult concerned with the strategy, and it does change inappropriate behaviour. It appears more damaging to the individual's pride, initially, than to the body.

However, there are a number of problems with this strategy. One is the physical demand on the person doing the holding. Women should normally hold females, and men males. It is time-consuming, especially since it can be required at the most inconvenient times, such as when meals are about to begin; or there may be no suitable staff around, or not enough to allow the holding to take place. Also the initial noise the youngster makes in their struggle to free themselves or gain control can be unnerving for others unaware of what is happening. Even if they are aware, it can be distressing.

When a resident physically assaults a staff member, very serious consideration is given as to whether or not that person can be allowed to stay on in the House. Where there has been evidence of provocation by a staff member, then this can be an ameliorating factor. It is very difficult if those who work with youth feel physically at risk in their job. For this reason, physical abuse of staff is grounds for dismissal.

Over the years it has become clear that violence, even from just one resident, can unsettle the whole House and make for widespread acting out. It is like one fire cracker setting off a whole lot of others. Most of the youngsters have lived with violent backgrounds for many years, and have sought an escape from that within our Homes. It seems that one violent resident acting out triggers off other people's neuroses, and there are real problems to deal with as a result.

The answer has been to create an environment that is affectionate, with plenty of caring, touching and respectful treatment of one another. It also means staff maintaining a calm stance and manner, so that the residents are able to respond to that, rather than an aggressive, loud approach. A further requirement is to ensure that each young person gets adequate, consistent attention. When this does not happen, then problem behaviours inevitably result.

Our policy for residents who use violence depends on the nature of the assault and to what extent it was provoked. Unprovoked attacks are followed up immediately by suspension, while the future of the aggressor is considered. He or she is usually placed temporarily in a different House; but if the attack is a serious one, the police are involved, charges are laid, and the person responsible may be placed in a welfare institution.

In cases where there is evidence of provocation by someone else, then the parties are brought together, degrees of responsibility are worked out, and appropriate consequences are decided on for either or both, as the case warrants. Angry and aggressive acts are part of most family life, unfortunately, so it is not surprising that we should experience these reactions in Houses with large groups of people who have been used to dealing with frustration through physical attacks.

Simon was a Maori youth who came to Greys Avenue when he was fourteen years old. For the first six months, he seemed to have little respect for me. When he got into trouble, he used to say to me, 'Hit me, go on, hit me!' When I answered that I did not believe in hitting people, he would reply with some scorn, 'What sort of head are you? Fathers have to hit, if they are the bosses. You are no good if you don't use capital (meaning corporal) punishment. You're no father.' He grew to think differently over the six years he lived with us.

When I have asked adults what we should do regarding 'pot' smoking among residents, the answers are varied. Many say there is nothing you can do about it, as its use is widespread in the community. It is a difficult problem, not so much because of its criminal connotations, but because of the psychological effects produced on the users. Most of our residents have emotional problems, and we have found over many years that marijuana exacerbates these.

Many youths in our care have not benefited the way we would have wished, because of their pre-occupation with smoking 'grass'. They are unable to concentrate at school or work, miss out on appointments, commit criminal acts under its influence, and develop a 'couldn't care less' attitude. Good resolutions about all kinds of changes in their lives last only until the next smoke, and then all resolutions go overboard. Many of them have admitted, at a later stage, that pot smoking was their undoing.

78

We had one girl who was warned about smoking marijuana and how fragile she was. These cautions were ignored and she ended up on one occasion directing traffic in a city street; on another she held up people with an air rifle for fun. In this case the armed offenders squad was called out, and the girl got a heavy custodial sentence. I think that cured her of her smoking behaviour.

Regarding drugs, it has always been our policy not to take heavy drug users who were still caught up with their habit. Special controlled facilities are needed if proper care is to be given to such people. Over the years we have had many who have given up drugs or nearly worked through their drug problems, and we have been able to provide a supportive environment for them. Some of our most successful rehabilitations have been with such young people.

We tell residents that marijuana is illegal and therefore cannot be allowed in or used in the Houses. We also require that staff do not use marijuana, since the models they present to residents are extremely important. Any dealing will be reported to the police, and there will be no support from the Houses if it is proven. From time to time we run educational programmes on drug abuse, but we try to be positive in our approach. We emphasise the importance of being concerned about what goes into one's body, and taking care of oneself.

On one occasion we found that a staff member, who had come to us well recommended, was using hard drugs, and her husband turned out to be a dealer. On occasion she invited a few residents around to her home, and allowed them to smoke pot there. It was not surprising she had considerable influence over some of the more difficult residents.

As soon as I found out what was going on, I went round to her home and dismissed her. But some damage continued after this. Not every resident could appreciate the grounds for her dismissal. I explained what had happened and the action I took. A few of her closest admirers revolted against the dismissal, and refused to co-operate in the House. Eventually they had to go too, as they continued in their drug activity. It took some months to recover from that disaster.

In more recent times, glue sniffing has become commonplace among the younger set. Few residents under seventeen coming to our Homes will not have tried sniffing. It is not, however, a problem within our Houses. We have so far managed to keep it in check, by the use of two things — peer pressure, and individual resolution of problems. Glue sniffing or solvent abuse are seen as childish and irresponsible behaviours by most residents, so there is no status to be gained from boasting of being a sniffer. Former glue sniffers have been very effective in persuading the newer residents who are users to give up the habit. As soon as the newcomer gains security in the House and gets individualised attention, a change takes place, and the former user rarely lapses.

Theft has increased in our society in recent years, and this is shown in the number of locks we now have to have on doors and cupboards. When we started, nothing was locked up; now most things are, as thieving becomes a way of life. A colleague of mine lives in a long Auckland suburban street, in which every house has been burgled, including his own — some several times. While videos have been the thief's bait, even those who don't own one cannot feel secure about their property. Manufacturers of burglar alarms have made a fortune, but have failed to stem the rise in thefts.

Many youngsters in need of residential care have been well schooled in the art of breaking and entering or car conversion. For quite a number, it has been a way of punishing their parents. Since none of our Homes are prisons or secure lock-ups, we have trouble making sure that this type of criminal behaviour ceases on arrival. Many of them will test us out at first by committing a crime, to see if we will react by expelling them.

In order to safeguard our neighbours and to try as much as possible to ensure our acceptance in an area, we have a policy of expelling anyone who steals from or seriously offends our close neighbours. This policy has been enforced several times. We co-operate with the police if they are trying to trace any stolen property or want to investigate a resident suspected of crime.

Internal theft is one of the great difficulties of all Houses such as ours. Some are expert in selling off other people's clothing to second-hand shops. It is a constant hassle trying to deal with this problem. Ex-residents can also create difficulties, by coming back at night and stealing goods from the Homes.

As a result of these problems, we have decided to have a set of ordinary wear clothes for younger residents which are shared. They are washed regularly, and a new issue is given out when the worn ones are handed in. Special individual 'going-out' clothes are kept under lock and signed for on issue. This has helped keep down the level of thieving. But all this taking from one another breeds insecurity and lack of trust, which spoil the atmosphere we are endeavouring to create.

When a resident is known to have thieved, internally or exter- nally, this is a matter for discussion with the entire House. Often the residents are left to deal with the matter on their own, under a senior responsible member's chairmanship. Consequences follow for such thieving. Where possible, we invite the victim to attend such a meeting, so that the consequences are brought home as strongly as possible.

A supportive programme exists for those who are known offenders. In intensive individual therapy, we try to unearth and deal with the reasons behind the criminal behaviour. One youth was a compulsive car converter, who had taken well over a hundred cars. As a smaller boy, he used to go to bed with a breadboard or something similar that could serve as an imaginary steering wheel. Our approach to him, and the only one that met with any success, was to help him buy his own car, and to become involved in maintaining it as well as driving it. It proved an effective, though expensive, approach to his problem!

Much thieving by young people is tied up with unsatisfactory family relationships. As in the case of solvent abuse, this is our primary area of attention in working with these problem behaviours. While we insist on restitution where possible, and suitable consequences for criminal behaviour, and the residents usually know or have their strong suspicions about who has taken goods from the Houses, proving it or getting the things back is extremely difficult.

Twice a year I lecture the students (graduate doctors and nurses) in the Obstetrics and Gynaecology Diploma Course. On one occasion I asked the group of seventy or so for their opinion as to what was the best way to deal with sexual relationships among residents. Most were in favour of allowing these to take place, provided there was an education programme and certain safeguards, such as contraceptives, freedom of choice and safeguards in terms of age.

More than most issues, we have had to argue this one through. Our policy is not to encourage close relationships among residents, and in fact to forbid sexual relationships among those living in a Youthlink Trust Home. While we enforce these rules as much as we can, we do not go prying, or act over punitively if the regulation is breached. We believe we are there to help youngsters in their development, and a most important aspect of this is their sexual needs. So we try to be positive and use all opportunities for teaching good human and sexual relationships.

Naturally, in Houses of the kind run by the Youthlink Trust, there are quite a number of minor requirements, such as not swearing at staff, taking off from the property without permission, or truanting from school. There tends to be a set way of dealing with such misdemeanours. Our policy is to attend to

81

misbehaviour as soon as possible, and to see that consequences follow immediately. These may include doing dishes, cleaning toilets or the kitchen, sweeping the drive or writing a letter of apology. Usually these consequences are overseen by a staff member or a senior resident.

If the behaviour is serious or the person is constantly misbehaving, they face the likelihood of demotion from the level they are in at the time. This is talked over by staff and brought up at the weekly residents' meetings. Failure to fulfill the consequence can lead to even tougher requirements, such as a supervised work crew all day on a weekend.

Consequences can be positive as well as punitive. Residents who have been especially helpful or made an outstanding contribution to the House may get special mention at a meeting, a pocket money bonus, or some special recognition or privilege. These are not linked with any given behaviour, but are efforts to acknowledge goodwill and helpfulness as well as a resident doing good things for themselves and others in their lives. Extra time spent with them, drives in a staff car, a meal out, or being given a special responsibility all help a resident learn that appropriate behaviour is recognised and attended to.

Residents whose names keep appearing on the negative consequences list come up for special attention at staff meetings. This usually takes the form of working out what is going wrong, and discussing ways of changing the direction the young person seems to be heading in. Sometimes such a resident is brought in before the whole staff at their meeting, and the concern is shared with him or her. All these are attempts to bring about better responses in the resident's attitudes and behaviours. As often as not they prove successful.

In all our Houses, regular group activities occur and are an integral part of changing undesirable behaviour and developing various skills. The groups differ in each of the Homes according to the age of occupants. Some groups and activities we run cover arts and crafts, including glass-painting, carving, weaving, sewing and canoe-making. There are also sports fixtures which encourage competition against oneself rather than others. The therapeutically orientated groups include those that train residents in self-assertiveness, confidence, communications skills and problem solving. There are also men's and women's groups that address specific sexist issues and raise awareness of these, so that there is a carry over into relations between the two sexes. We also have cultural groups and general groups dealing with individual problems.

Most of these groups have defined lives of six to ten weeks, with a commitment from residents to them for that period. Some groups are compulsory, but most are voluntary. Usually they are held at the Houses, though some take place at the Crisis Centre. We also take residents out to specific courses such as jazzercise, dancing and carpentry, and we occasionally enrol residents individually in courses such as piano tuition or athletics.

These groups and activities are constantly reviewed and developed to meet the needs of the residents at the time. Personnel from the Crisis Centre, from outside resources, and from the staff help to run these programmes. Consistency becomes a problem at times, with residents leaving before a group is finished, staff unable to attend for various reasons, or some members stopping coming to the activity. However, we try to keep them going.

(6)
Working with Families

It took me many years in adolescent care to appreciate the importance to disturbed or rejected young people of their family. I was aware that no one can replace parents fully in the care of young people, but I did not appreciate the need to work consistently and patiently with mothers and fathers who were estranged from their children or unable to control them. I too readily believed the child's negative comments about parents, or theirs about each other, and did not arrange sufficient opportunities for reconciliations to come about. Family therapy is in fact a recent approach to helping parents and families to live together or understand each other in a way that is not destructive to anyone concerned.

Limited resources, and the heavy demands from many needy youngsters, also made it difficult to maintain steady communication with families. Over the years, most left it to us to make contact with them about their child. For some time I had urged our staff to keep parents informed about their child, and make them welcome. We had tried having 'parent Sundays', when parents of youth in care would meet with several of us, and we would offer support through discussion and from mothers and fathers hearing of other parents' problems. This seemed to make them feel less guilty and more appreciative of their son or daughter.

However, the residents did not like us having their parents over, mainly because only a few attended, and they were either embarrassed because their parents *had* shown up, or resented the fact they did *not* come, and became depressed as a result. Gradually we gave up on that approach as the numbers dwindled and the residents' opposition was strong. We tried holding meetings with individual parents at the Houses, but the same problems persisted. At this stage we did not have the Crisis Centre rooms, where all family therapy meetings are now held. These are away from the gaze of other residents, and are free of distractions.

The advent of much younger residents than we had previously cared for has meant that more parents are willing to be involved. Our policy has also changed, in that we now set a high priority on family involvement. People have responded to this and tend to take it for granted more than before, especially when they find that we are sympathetic to their needs and listen to their side of the problem.

The parental form opposite lists what Youthlink commits itself

to in assisting a family and what is expected from the family in
return. The Trust's obligation is to provide accommodation, care,
supervision, any necessary therapy, contact with the family and a
plan for the future of the young person. The family is asked to
work in with the Trust's programme, attend family sessions, keep

---

YOUTHLINK AND PARENT FORM

The YOUTHLINK TRUST very much believes in the principle that the
most important individuals in a young person's life are her or his
parents. With that in mind we would like to establish the following commitment on both sides.

The YOUTHLINK TRUST *commits itself to assisting* . . . .
. . . . in their development and family relations by:

- Providing accommodation, care and supervision;
- Counselling and therapy as may be deemed necessary;
- A caring environment, that involves respect for the resident's
  needs, including emotional ones;
- Regular communication with the resident's parent(s);
- Opportunities for the resident and her or his family to meet
  on formal (therapy) or informal occasions;
- A plan for the resident to progress to returning home or to
  another suitable living situation when that is appropriate.

The Family of . . . . *commits itself to assisting by*:

- Working in with the plans for our youth's wellbeing;
- Attend whatever family sessions that may be planned and that
  endeavour to fit in with family responsibilities and timetables;
- Keep the Trust informed of any behaviours or changes either
  on our youth's or family's side;
- Support the Trust's efforts to assist our family member;
- Share any concerns, satisfactions or criticisms with responsible
  staff;
- Pay $. . . . . per week to assist in the expenses involved.
- I/We appoint the Administrator of The Home in which
  . . . . will live, to act in my absence and in
  emergencies as my child's guardian, on the understanding that
  the Trust Officer will consult where at all possible in all
  matters of importance concerning my/our youth.

Signed: . . . . (Parent(s))
. . . .
. . . . (Trust)
Date: . . . .

---

in touch with the staff working with the youth, and contribute what they can to the upkeep of the family member. (No youth is turned away because of lack of finances.) The family sessions are held at times to suit their convenience.

We have found that it is possible for residential homes to work co-operatively and well with the families of those living in care. In most cases the initial relationship is tentative, often there can be resentment against us, as we are sometimes seen as taking their child away from them, or they fear we may succeed where they haven't. We point out in these cases that any success we have will depend on family co-operation as well as on the young person's efforts. It soon becomes clear to families that we appreciate them, and that it is a combined partnership that is called for.

A working relationship between families and residential homes is not easy to establish. The history of relations between residential care and the home the child has come from has often not been good in the past. Nowadays this is changing. It has also been found that it is better to use gentle persuasion to get a family to seek help, rather than use coercion through statutory bodies such as Social Welfare. But sometimes this does not work, and because of the risk to the child, the law has to intervene.

There are various ways in which a partnership can be established between families and therapy or residential programmes for the young. It is easiest when the parents seek such help, because then there is a willingness to fit in with what is offered. The vital links are established at the first meeting, where parents make judgements concerning trust, confidence and willingness to listen to what is said. So the skills of the interviewer and his or her sensitive approach are paramount for a harmonious relationship. Even when the qualities for a good working relationship are not present initially, it is possible, with time, to win people over. This particularly occurs when therapy sessions give all concerned insight into what is happening and ways of bringing about change.

A family is larger than child, mother and father. The brothers and sisters are also important and have their contribution to make to giving insight into what is going on in a family, and how they are affected. So sessions should include as many members of the family as possible. In many cases, the child will be returning home, and will certainly have ongoing contact with the family; therefore all members should be aware of what is happening. It also helps to take away the idea that the child in care is to blame or is solely responsible for the difficulties the family is having.

Anyone who has attended family therapy sessions will be aware of the striking insights even young children can have as to what is going on in their family. Their perceptions are vital.

Usually the parents find the therapy sessions easier than the young person in care, in whom we often find an ambivalence. They are aware of the good that is being done through the sessions, and that these may help a speedier return home, but they are scared of parental reactions. 'Will Dad hit me like he always does when I say things that he doesn't like?' 'I don't want to hear Mum and Dad shouting at each other again like they always do!' 'I know they will blame me for everything that has gone wrong.' 'I'm scared that they will split up, the way things are going.' These are some of the pre-session comments one hears. Sometimes on the day therapy is due, the youngster will run away (the session still goes on), or will misbehave in a serious way. Often too there will be reactions after the therapy, such as smashing windows, getting drunk, or committing some crime. The young person will do these things because of the stress all are going through trying to improve the family communication. As hurts are brought to the surface, it is natural for the young person to act out in a strong and negative way. Trying to contain such situations is difficult, and it is important for the person to be able to vent feelings; but finding appropriate ways for this to happen is not easy.

The ideal is to be able to work with both parents as well as with the other members of a family. With the large number of single parent families and the remoteness of the absent parent, it is often difficult to achieve an integrated approach involving the whole family, but this does not make the situation impossible. An example of this was a youth whose mother was dead.

The first time I ever heard of Warwick was in a letter from a counsellor who had dealt with the family and was at a loss as to how to help the fifteen-year-old boy. There had been tragedy in the family: his mother had had to cope with severe asthmatic attacks, and her long stay in hospital, as well as the father having to look after the four young children while trying to keep his job, had affected the boy's upbringing. The climax for him was seeing his mother fall gasping to the floor in front of him, shuddering, then lying immobile on the ground. It was some time before he realised his mother was dead. The memory stayed with him to haunt him at times, and a sense of guilt persisted that he could somehow have saved her, if he had done 'the right thing' and gone for help.

The father did his best to cope, but it was extremely stressful for him. The eldest daughter ran away from home; the next eldest child, a boy, became involved in drugs and dealing in them, and ended up in jail. The distressed father became ill, due to excessive nervous strain, and became a house-bound invalid. He found it incredibly hard to cope with the younger son, who seemed very influenced by his elder brother and took more notice of him, even though the youth was in prison, than he did of his father. In many ways he felt ashamed of his Dad; he resented not having a mother, and the invalid condition of his father.

Warwick had been involved in a lot of borderline criminal activity, but had never been sentenced, only admonished by the Courts, for his behaviour. But the gap had grown between the youth and his father and he was truanting from school ('I am fifteen and you can't make me go!'), and he had taken to threatening his father, at times almost striking him. He was aware of the fear he provoked in his sick parent.

The school counsellor who wrote to me about this youth was concerned for his future and the father's safety. He asked me to see the boy and perhaps provide accommodation. This was arranged, and Warwick moved into Rowan House. The week before he arrived he had walked out of the school, even though he had got on well with the woman counsellor there. The school itself was a fairly open one, offering a wide variety of subject choices.

Warwick was reluctant to see me, as he protested that he 'didn't want to see any shrink'. He warmed to me somewhat when I offered him a chance of a break from home, and when he learnt that he did not have to go back to school as a condition of his moving into the House. He soon came to enjoy the company of the other residents, and said that he had been bored at home with his father, who (he said) watched a lot of television and did not talk to him very much.

This youth was still pliant enough to respond to some of the more positive influences in the House. We tried to take care that he did not associate only with those of similar behaviours to himself. One of the more difficult moves was to get Warwick to change his admiration for his brother's criminal activities. He felt the ultimate for him was to be a jailbird like his brother and mix with the types that had hung around with him.

As is usual for all residents, a therapeutic programme was planned for and with Warwick. In such situations we look at the person's needs, set goals to meet these, and provide the support to make progress with the tasks that have been set. While counselling or therapy of some kind is usually a part of such planning, it is not the only thing that will help bring about change. The important aspects are the day-to-day activities and experiences that help young people see where they had been heading, and how to effect change.

So the therapy for Warwick was to help him look at his guilt and grief over his mother, get his brother into perspective, examine his own level of self-esteem, work on his anger with his father, and learn how to express his emotions without feeling weak or embarrassed. Soon the youth became more aware of his need for support and actively sought out the counsellor. Regular sessions were held and the youth knew that within a defined timetable, he had an opportunity to face up to some of the more painful things about himself and his life.

While these interventions were helpful, and ultimately enjoyed by the youth, they were only effective because of the fact that he was separated from his old pattern of living and the stress of being with his father, he had the evidence of others similar to himself working through emotional problems, and had a structured environment which he had to come to terms with. After nine months of effort, including quite a number of setbacks, Warwick had got to the stage where he was willing to meet with his father in a counselling session.

The meeting was a tense one. The sick man found it difficult to get his breath, and was clearly agitated. We took the session at a quiet level, concentrating on what Warwick had achieved rather than his past misbehaviour (which his father kept bringing up). It was important to make this first session as positive as possible, so that the meetings could continue. This proved possible, and in future sessions we made real progress. It was not possible to have other members of the family present, so we made do. Sometimes we got the youth to imagine his mother was sitting in the empty chair and to address issues relating to her. We did similar things in relation to his brother.

After the second meeting, Warwick felt able to spend a weekend at home, and his father was happy to try that out. It worked well and the periods spent at home with his father increased. He had been able to get out his anger against his father in therapy. But he also was able to hear things from his father's viewpoint and appreciate what he had been trying to do. He also came to accept his father's illness and became supportive rather than angry and ashamed about him. Eventually Warwick returned home. We had one more therapy session after that, which was a brief one, and as far as I know the relationship has continued to be good and Warwick has made good progress in his life.

This is not a text on family therapy, so the various techniques and theories are not relevant to this text. What is important is the value of such an approach in helping people to change their perceptions and ways of relating, to a degree that improves their own and their family's quality of life. So very often, a family discovers that when the 'problem child' leaves home, all is not resolved, and often another member becomes a difficulty. Another common occurrence is that therapy reveals the fractured relationship between the parents. Often this can be rectified through help offered to the couple separately from the full family sessions.

We have had some families who do not wish to accept that their son or daughter is not the one 'to blame' for the family stresses, and they have dropped out of therapy. We make efforts, after a space of time, to bring them back into the counselling sessions. Therapy is expensive of time, in that families often change the appointment date at the last minute. Two out of three families do this, for a variety of reasons.

As a result of one of the Telethons held in New Zealand, the Trust in 1985 received funding to employ for the first time, for a year, a full-time trained family therapist. Bill Ivory was appointed and has written on aspects of his work for this chapter.

I have decided to concentrate on three specific issues, which seem to me crucial and relevant to the families of Youthlink residents and they are also true of any family.

1) *The tragic consequences of society's willingness to blame parents when children become troublesome, or for that matter to blame children;*

2) *The process of grief in action with families who are separated from one or more of their children;*

3) *The importance of a 'family approach' to families in trouble.*

In my previous work as a Family Therapist, I was employed by a church agency, which had a division specialising in family care. In that work by far the greater number of families seen were those experiencing difficulties beyond their own resources to cope, and this was the first time they had sought help. In Youthlink, the families I see have been seeking help for two or more years, and usually have been to many agencies without success. In all cases, Youthlink families present as having accepted negative and highly derogatory labels, for either their parents or their children.

Sometimes these labels are imposed implicitly, but most often they are explicit, and by people who professionally should have known better. Social workers, psychiatrists, general practitioners, psychologists and counsellors are all represented among those blamed. *The tragedy that stems from this 'mad or bad' labelling is that it inevitably paralyses families and furnishes them evidence that change or improvement is impossible.* I have no quarrel with professionals who need to have names for people with problems as a means of understanding and martialling the appropriate resources and planning treatment, but to impose their labels on family members is unnecessary and dangerous.

Rosa was thirteen years old when I met her, but she looked more like a ten year old. She was an only child. Intellectually gifted, she was a year ahead at school of her age group. Her parents were very concerned that Rosa was displaying 'all the signs of clinical depression'. They knew this because they had both been clinically depressed for years until being 'cured' through psychotherapy. They wished me to do psychotherapy on their daughter so that she too might be 'cured'. Their description of the behaviours that concerned them were all the behaviours of any group of adolescents.

What bothered them was Rosa's constant arguing with them, her sulking for long periods, when denied her own way and temper tantrums when asked to tidy her room. Her parents responded to her sulking periods with hours of pleading, comforting and trying to discover 'what was going on inside her'. They had labelled her sulking as the beginnings of chronic depression. Their personal twelve years of misery and anti-depressant drugs quite naturally made them want something different for their daughter. Psychotherapy had cured them so it should also cure their child.

It is understandable that this family, after a long succession of experts telling them their symptoms meant clinical depression, requiring control by drugs, should have no confidence in their own resources for change. It was the side-effects of the drugs they were taking that led them to seek a possible alternative solution. It is also easy to appreciate how psychotherapy had become important in their thinking. After all it had liberated them from years of drug taking. However, is a psychotherapy, which only removes or relieves symptoms, really any better than drugs, which have the same results? Apart from the obvious physical benefits, I do not think so.

Rosa's parents appeared as dependent on psychotherapy as they once were on medication. As long as they remained dependent on anything outside of themselves, they would remain ignorant of their personal resources for change, and would be denied the opportunity of changes that would ultimately empower them to cope better with future problems. This all started because once a doctor told them that they were 'clinically depressed'. This provided them with a rational explanation for all their unhappiness and a prescription for helplessness to change.

In families, what parents believe their child to be, that child usually

91

will fulfil the expectation or try to. When I met Rosa, she was beginning to try quite convincingly, to portray all the symptoms her parents had told her they were frightened she would develop.

Max, aged fourteen years, had been residing in a Youthlink Home for two years. He came to us after considerable trouble with the police and school for stealing. At the time he arrived at Youthlink, he had become a State Ward. He had not attended school for the previous year and was often brought home late at night by the police. His parents had tried to control him but now admitted that he was beyond their care, even though they had sought help from many agencies. Max had two younger brothers and an elder sister, all of whom caused no trouble. The family were very distressed that Max had to be placed in care. I became involved, when it was reported to me that Max had been two years in Youthlink and for six months had been no problem. It was thought he should return home.

When I entered the interviewing room where the family were seated, I sensed a great tension, as if a bomb was about to go off. It took two hours of gentle questioning before I realised what had happened. When the family had signed over to Social Welfare their rights over their son, to them he had died, and he felt he had also. Physically he had lived on, but emotionally they all felt dead. During the two years Max had been 'in care', he and his family, in their separate ways, had been grieving. His family had built a new life without him and the same went for his own life. The 'untriggered bomb' they felt was about to go off, was that I would impose a reunion on them, and they would be forced to face the risk of going through all the past torment again.

The parents talked a great deal about all the help they had sought when their son was at home. Nothing had worked and they believed they had been made to feel 'bad parents'. This feeling came through to them, even though they had other children who were doing well. The one problem child labelled them 'bad'.

Apart from a similarity of labelling processes, that were part of Rosa's story, this case illustrates how a grieving process begins automatically in families, when separation is forced on them. This is not a major problem, if there is no intention to reunite the parties. If there is any possibility of a future coming together, then it is necessary to address this issue at the time of fostering. After taking a child away from his or her parents, and exposing them to the inevitable grief that follows, it is an injustice to then propose a reunion, expecting them to go through the risk of the same grieving again.

Johnathan came to Youthlink from one of the larger metropolitan cities in New Zealand. He had exhausted the resources of every social agency, foster home, psychologist and counsellor in the area. His reported problems were dressing up in women's clothing and truanting from school. Shortly after entering one of our residential homes, it was revealed in a *case conference, that he was exhibiting none of his former problems. The next question was why had he been sent to us in the first instance and what was behind the concern expressed in the documents accompanying his arrival.*

Eventually, I escorted Johnathan back to his home city to meet with his family in order to gain some insight into our dilemma. Two trips and four family sessions later, Johnathan's six-year-old brother eventually revealed the secret — incest (sexual activity with both parents). We had talked about many problems the family had endured for years, with no clue as to what was going on. Finally, the emotion generated by asking all the family to say goodbye to Johnathan was too much for the little brother and he blurted out the secret.

I had known, that in the four years that Johnathan had been in trouble, no professional involved had ever seen the whole family together. Family therapists believe, that when one member of a family is troubled, then by definition, every member is. Another way of expressing that reality, is to say that problems occur in a social context, and are best studied within that setting. Johnathan's problems occurred in his social context, his family. It took four meetings within that framework, before a way to understand his problems was revealed. While in Johnathan's case this understanding meant the unlikelihood of his returning home again, it also provided the information we needed to provide more appropriate support.

In all the years I have been counselling, I have yet to meet a parent who deliberately went out of their way to destroy their child's life. But I have met parents who were in fact destroying their children's lives. It would have been easy to have labelled them mad or bad or both, but that would have achieved nothing. I believe that by affirming the intentions behind what they were doing, the vital first step has been taken toward helping them guide in a loving, healthy and effective way, their children through the difficulties of adolescence.

Reading Bill Ivory's comments above reminds me how easily in the past I have not fully appreciated the hurt parents can feel, when a youth comes into our care. It is easy to note the child's distress because you are faced with it in introducing him or her into the residential home, while you can be misled by the seeming relief parents can display, when they feel a problem is being lifted from their shoulders. We try to put into practice the following policy in relation to parents and their son or daughter.

First, separation should only be a last resort or as temporary as possible. Therefore we try to offer support to a family so that the young person can continue living with them. When that fails or is impossible, then we consider residential placement. We take the

93

approach that the family *will* co-operate, rather than they might. We also try to take away a lot of the guilt feelings that parents bring to the placement of their child with others. They are made to feel welcome to remain involved with their child.

There are times, however, when this has to be restricted or even forbidden. Such a case would be where there has been sexual abuse, and the youth refuses at this stage to have any contact with the parent involved. It would also be appropriate to restrict contact where a child has become too dependent on or dominated by a parent to the extent that they are deeply affected in their development by this. Family therapy sessions are open to parents, and on our side, actively encouraged. We also endeavour not to talk disparagingly about parents with the child, or encourage the child to do so with us.

Family therapy sessions often break through some of the communication barriers and can allow a youth to visit home more frequently without the usual confrontations wrecking the relationship. Often these visits are at weekends, and are increased after consultations on both sides, speeding up eventual return home or to a flat. Those youngsters who have no parents, or are unable to relate to them in any worthwhile manner, receive special affection and attention to try and replace some of the emotional gaps that are there through parental lack.

We have had people whose parents have left them with us and effectively got lost in Australia, America or England, and no amount of sleuthing can find them. One mother gave her son $40 the afternoon she flew out of Auckland to Britain, and it was months before she sent back word of where she was. At fifteen he did not cope well with that rejection. Often the boy would protest to me that his mother wanted him over there with her, and why were we stopping him going? I read some of the letters which, he said, showed she wanted him. They were full of admonitions and warnings about keeping out of trouble. Here and there was an expression of regret that he wasn't in England with her, but no practical suggestions about what would happen if he arrived ('of course we only have a tiny flat in London, because housing is so expensive, so you would not be able to stay with us'), and no ticket to get him over there. Without any income he could not get himself over, and his mother knew that, so she was safe in making vague suggestions about his joining her. He just did not want to hear when we tried to confront him with reality.

Young people like that boy are in need of parenting, and staff have to provide it while the youth is in care. Others need what is often referred to as 'reparenting'. This expression is not the best for describing how one attempts to assist youngsters living away from home. There are only one or two people that a young person will acknowledge as parents, and they will be the strong influences in that person's life, no matter how much anger or rejection may be going on. For periods of time other adults can enter into such relationships, and can have a powerful influence, but ultimately it will be their own parents they will seek out. You cannot be a parent to another person's child unless you take full responsibility for them through adoption or a life-long commitment.

Often a child who has lacked sustained and systematic parental care, and is said to need reparenting, is in fact in need of parenting *per se*, as this has not been a feature of their life. So reparenting is not so much a substitute for birth-parents, as giving to a child or youth an experience of security, through consistent and sensitive relating in a continuing manner by a caring adult. This person acts in the child's life as a confidant, guide, teacher and buffer.

It is hard to maintain these characteristics in relating to a number of such children in need, who are hurt and make a point of trying to hurt or reject those trying to get close or be caring. If the youngster has been out of control or inappropriately dominating their family, this factor has to be worked on early in the relationship. If parents have not acted together or ensured that the children's or family's needs were met, then the child will try to maintain control in the new situation. So often a struggle will exist between the new acting parent(s) and the youngster to discover and establish who will be in charge. The young person ultimately resents any adults who allow them to get away with breaking the rules or the boundaries set up. While the child will try to wear the adult down by constant arguing and nagging, he will not appreciate, let alone be helped by, any giving-in by the parent figure.

We had a fourteen-year-old girl, Monica, who had lots of personality and confidence. We had placed her at Rowan House with the older age group when she first arrived, since there was no vacancy at The Glade at the time. She also appeared a much more mature person than her age would suggest.

A lot of anger and fieriness was in her behaviour and she tested the Rowan House staff to the limits. Drinking, pot smoking, the odd theft, were all part of her excitement in living — understandable, given parents who had been involved in crime (her father was in jail). We often told her that we thought we had made a mistake in placing her with the older residents as she clearly needed more restrictions on her behaviour than were operating at the House. I told her I felt she should be at The Glade with girls and boys her own age. She would cry and plead with us to give her another chance.

Another chance would be effective for about a day, then away Monica went on behaviours that had all the staff at odds with her. One day we decided it was enough. The Rowan House staff talked it over and we weighed the possible consequences, if we shifted her against her will to The Glade. Her therapist pointed out that since leaving her parents or being taken from them at eight years of age, she had never lasted anywhere for more than a few months, nor bonded with those looking after her. Would these good results of her stay be destroyed?

It was clear that the change had to be made, and when I informed Monica of our decision, she cried and begged for another chance. Hard as I found it, I said no. Shortly afterwards I took her by car to The Glade. On the way over, in front of two other residents from Rowan Road, I was interested, pleased and somewhat amazed to have Monica say to me, 'You know I am glad yous guys did what you did and said I had to go to The Glade. You know I was hoping you would say that I had to, but I had to fight you as much as I could.' She settled in well, had her moments, but became much more a girl of her age, and seemed more at peace.

So-called 'difficult children' are those who have learnt to behave in ways that are anti-social, irritating, or non-communicative. They are often resentful of their parents' perceived failures toward them, or their seeming rejection of them, or that they have broken up their relationship. Many carry a burden of guilt about their parents. They tend to act out their feelings through criminal, negative or non-coping behaviours. Some are extremely strong-minded, and struggle to fend off what they consider are threats to their survival or integrity. Not unlike them are what are called 'children at risk'. These are youngsters who have experienced some privations or who lack stability within their family. They become vulnerable to pressures from those they associate with, leading to crime, drugs, truancy or rejection of parental values.

The strategies used include attitudes as well as practical actions. One of the points that needs to be kept in mind is that it takes a lot of time and patience to win the trust of a child who feels rejected by her or his parents. So we take the building up of the relationship slowly, not forcing the person to talk when they don't want to or are not ready to do so. It is helpful to share with the youngster the motives one has for being involved in their life.

We encourage an insistence on those things that are seen as

essential for bringing up the child. For example, some of them have been used to going to bed or getting up when it suited them, and will struggle against a set bed-time. Since our involvement will normally only be for a short time, and also because it is damaging to the young person, we avoid possessiveness over the child.

When we least expect it these reticent youngsters will suddenly start talking and reveal many things about themselves. These will be the times when they will share hurts and feelings long hidden. One should never delay these disclosures to suit one's convenience. The youth expects the adult to be open in the relationship and not to engage in pleading or bribery in order to gain compliance. They will despise these manipulative tactics, though they may well try them on the adult. One of their big lacks has been consistency, so this is a prerequisite in helping needy youth.

Some of our more difficult residents have responded well to regular sessions with one, or two together, of our counsellors. If these meetings are set up, the counsellor must make them a priority and insist they happen. When behaviour has been especially bad, a resident can make significant changes by such supportive therapy. It is not an escape from responsibilities, but a means of gaining insight into what is happening in their life and having support to make changes. Therapy alone does not effect change, but has an important role when it is backed by an environment that is also therapeutic.

The therapy in structured sessions cannot be at odds with what is happening within the residential setting. So staff, programmes and ways of treating the young must be consistent, or the undermining can be totally destructive. In any residential setting, watchdogs have to be around constantly checking that the environment is itself therapeutic and conducive to healing and change. It must also recognise the primacy of family membership and work toward healing and strengthening those basic ties.

(7)
Making it Work

Since the start of the Youthlink operation in 1971, Government social policy in New Zealand for the care of needy or problem children and young people has changed. The State has gradually moved away from residential care of young people, closing down many of its hostels which catered for a variety of children's needs, and retaining only those homes that deal mainly with criminal behaviour by the young. With a few exceptions, the Department of Social Welfare has relied on encouraging adoption or fostering in private homes for those youngsters without permanent homes. It has also given support to private or church-based agencies such as ours, which provide places for more difficult or special needs cases.

When I was involved in setting up the Youthline Phone Counselling Service in 1969, there was only Lifeline operating in Auckland. Now there are new phone counselling services being set up every year to meet specific needs. While some are for abused children and women, others serve to meet emergency needs or to promote the religious aims of churches. Eleven emergency services are currently listed at the front of the Auckland telephone directory. Similarly, youth hostels have multiplied over the same period. Whenever there is a public outcry about street kids or glue sniffers, new homes may be opened to meet these problems.

Over the past fifteen years, there have been many such initiatives, but most have not lasted the distance. Financial problems, abuse of the home by residents, exhaustion from the degree of energy required to run such homes, lack of appreciation, and no clear understanding about exactly what the overseers of some of the homes were trying to do, have contributed to the failure of these projects. In order to maintain a relevant service, it is also essential to be aware of current or changing needs, and adapt to meet them. In Youthlink I have tried to keep a close watch on changing patterns of problems and needs, and to respond to these through the services offered. These attempts have usually been limited because of constraints on finance or the other resources available.

At the time of writing, this is the first occasion we have had a guarantee of sufficient resources to carry out the work of adolescent care in a way that can ensure competent staff and consistent operation of programmes. This presents both a burden and a challenge. There is much more accountability required when a venture is funded; but that is a burden I am happy to live with, after years of trying to function on a totally inadequate budget and constant uncertainty about staff numbers and quality.

Youthlink owes a great deal to Government support for various *ad hoc* developments during the last fifteen years. This has included the provision of two large properties at nominal rent by the Departments of Social Welfare and Justice, and the staffing provided by funds from the Labour Department through its various employment schemes. The Education Department has also assisted through encouragement in the development of our educational programme.

There have been both traps and advantages in some of that assistance. The traps lay in building up a very large organisation on the shaky basis of insecure funding and staffing. The fact that we were able to achieve so much with such limited resources was a good argument for better Government funding for the Trust. Over the last four years we have grown from one Home and six staff with thirty-five youths to four Houses, a Crisis Centre, a school, seventy residents and over thirty staff. While such growth is too rapid to be desirable, it nevertheless represented long-term planning and opportunities to be grasped. Presently we are involved in a process of consolidation.

Sometimes as I sit at meetings and hear administrative staff bemoaning the lack of sufficient staff numbers, and making comparisons with statutory agencies, I think back to the earlier days of the project, when two or three volunteers made it work with twenty-three residents. I then have to remind myself that times have changed: the problems are different, and a much larger degree of accountability and professionalism is demanded now. Though I understand their point, I get nervous when staff make comparisons with state-run facilities, since they are not our model. If our youth care becomes only a job, and the level of wages is the prime factor for people working with us, then I believe we will lose the basis for the start of Youthlink, the loving care of young people in need.

Unlike state-run institutions, we have a measure of freedom to operate in our own way and without the constraints common to such homes. There is the opportunity to put more time and energy into the youth, and become more involved with them. Not that all these things automatically or necessarily happen; nor is this a criticism of the care and concern of those working in State institutions. The possibilities are simply greater in community-run homes.

Once the Homes were staffed entirely by volunteers; now most staff are full-time and are paid. Where workers originally gave much more than forty hours a week, most now work the standard hours only. This is in keeping with the times, where living expenses are heavy and people expect to be paid as a sign that what they do is valued. In the past five years, we have relied heavily on unemployment schemes for most of our staff and their wages. In times of high unemployment, new staffing schemes were readily approved, but they were slow to be actioned when the labour market was healthier. The more unemployed, the greater the selection we had to choose from. At the peak of the Voluntary Organisation Training Programme (VOTP) scheme, we were employing twenty-two workers. While some excellent people have come to work with us through these schemes, we have also been forced, through lack of alternatives, to employ some staff who proved more of a hindrance than a help.

At times highly skilled people have come through the Labour Department, but in most cases they lacked experience, and certainly had not worked with difficult or disturbed adolescents. As time went on changes were made in Departmental requirements. These included greater time spent in training, with close supervision on an individual basis, and much more paper work and careful dotting of the 'i's in applications for staff. One of the greatest problems was keeping pace with the changes in staff within the Department itself. A good rapport would no sooner be established with an officer, and things begin to flow, than that person would leave or be shifted to another position. So we experienced long delays, different standards or requirements, and hold-ups in staff replacements.

There was also the constant fear that a worker would leave before the completion of the year's work period. Many did, and one could not blame them — they preferred a secure job to possible future employment. Then we would have to start training a fresh recruit. We would have liked to keep some trainees, but had no funding to do so. Sacking a worker was a problem too, in that there would be long delays before any replacement was made, or worse still, the scheme would be cancelled. Usually we would learn about this some months after the worker had left.

Some of the things that we often had to overlook were consistent lateness for work (a real problem when the good order of a large home depends on staff punctuality), taking days off without sufficient reason, taking away food belonging to the House (e.g. frozen meat or tins of coffee) and failure to attend training programmes.

What we did not overlook, no matter what the consequences, were any sexual or criminal activities. An example of such behaviour was a worker who one night got into bed with a young woman. He was dressed only in his underclothing, and she pushed him out. Later, when I investigated this, he offered the excuse that the resident was provocative. This was certainly true of her previous record, but was in no way accepted as an excuse. I told him that this was all the more reason for staff making sure such a girl was safe in our Homes, and he was dismissed. I was appalled to learn that he had returned the same evening and involved some residents in drinking with him and trying to gain their sympathy, saying that he had been badly treated. As soon as he heard that I was on my way over to deal with him, he took off. This was the kind of problem that could arise in having to employ people who were not much older than some of the youth they were meant to be helping.

When staff are employed, they must read the special manual written for them. It outlines the behaviour required, such as being punctual, keeping to rostered times or arranging a satisfactory replacement, involving themselves with the residents, and setting a good standard of personal behaviour as a model.

The manual also stresses that it is utterly essential for success in our work that we are united as a team. This means learning to respect each other and our different strengths, being honest and sharing our concerns, not undermining each other, including in front of other staff or residents, and supporting each other. Trying to see the positive aspects of each person we are involved with and recognising their strengths as opposed to being preoccupied with their weaknesses, is important.

Staff are asked to accept that cleanliness is a sign of what is happening within the operation and individual lives, so it is a priority for all, whatever their brief in the system. Bribery and rewards for specific tasks or compliances are not part of our philosophy and are to be avoided. Recognition of individuals for what they are in themselves is vital. Threatening residents with expulsion or suspensions as a consequence for actions is not part of our approach. This differs from reminding youths of their responsibilities and the normal consequences that follow from certain behaviours.

The grounds for dismissal of staff are also set out. It states that if the behaviour listed is proven, then a staff member will be immediately dismissed. The unacceptable actions listed include sexual activity in or out of the House with a resident, virtually any activity involving drugs, unprovoked violence, and consistent non-attendance at work.

Over the years I have had to investigate many an accusation by residents or other staff about unacceptable staff behaviour. Sometimes a resident is out to get rid of a person they dislike or are presently angry with, and eventually this is unearthed. There have been occasions when residents have boasted to their peers about what has happened with a certain staff member, in order to enhance their mana. When such false accusations are discovered, the resident has to face whatever consequences are thought appropriate. It is very stressful for an innocent staff member to have to cope with such accusations. They are aware that every complaint or rumour of misbehaviour in serious matters will be thoroughly investigated.

There have been several cases where a rather disturbed young person has misinterpreted innocent gestures by a staff member as a sexual advance. Most of these have been so interpreted weeks or months after they actually occurred. Some find it hard to separate fact from fiction in their lives, and genuinely believe they were assaulted or that a staff member intended to assault them. These cases take some sorting out.

One mother notified me that her son had laid a complaint against a staff member, and this was a major reason why he did not wish to return to the House. We held a conference with the youth, his mother, our family therapist, the accused staff member and myself. It eventuated that there had been no suggestion of a sexual act by the staff member, but only a playful holding action in the hallway in front of many residents. The youth was eventually able to own his reasons for misinterpreting the action, and the need for him to separate fact from fiction. It clearly had suited him to gather reasons for being allowed to stay at home. This was made possible without his having to concoct excuses relating to the House.

While staff members have been exonerated on many such occasions, the individual accused can go through great stress in the process. Those who are in the wrong are instantly dismissed. Stories can also be exaggerated or passed among staff and residents at times. When this happens it can be very damaging to the atmosphere of a House and the good of the Trust as a whole. I have found that there are quite a number of people who seem pleased to learn of any scandal or weakness in the Trust.

While residents are encouraged to notify senior staff or their

Special Person of any untoward behaviour by a staff member, they are also warned of the seriousness of false accusations. I personally involve myself in all such situations and endeavour to discover the truth. On occasions when I have felt the issue was unclear, I have invited the police to make an assessment of the problem. In all such cases, no guilt by staff was established.

Early in 1985, one of our long term staff members went to Australia for a weekend break. Diana had been a senior staff member; years before, she spent quite a few years in therapy as she worked through her own drug problem. In the five years with us, there had been no evidence of any lapses back into drug abuse. However, when Diana died on the night of her arrival in Sydney, a number of rumours were spread concerning her behaviour and the cause of death. Word went out that she had died of a drug overdose.

At her memorial service in Auckland (being an Australian, she was buried in her country of birth), I drew attention to these insinuations and stated my faith in Diana and my belief that she had died from natural causes. It was months before the medical reports were available to confirm this. In the meantime her family, our staff and supporters had to live with the gossip and slur on our operation that the innuendo had generated.

Eventually I was able to forward to those most closely concerned an extract from the autopsy on Diana, and a letter from her mother which stated that Diana's file was now closed. Her mother said how much she had appreciated the service, and went on: 'We are proud of her achievements and grateful that you gave her the opportunities to develop her special skills and abilities — to the reward of both it seems.'

Within the Trust's senior staff there is a wealth of experience and expertise to call on for the formation of skilled workers with youth. The problem is to find the time on the job to ensure that staff get to attend such sessions. The demands of residents do not automatically stop because the staff are trying to upgrade their skills. Some staff find it difficult to follow the personal involvement that any good training programme for youth workers requires. It is easy for them to find a hundred other things to do at such times.

The Training Programme we operated in 1985 gives an idea of the areas that are stressed in helping workers learn to deal with the needs of young people with difficulties. In New Zealand and Australia, major issues are now coming to the fore which affect working with young people, their families and agencies. These concern racism and sexism. In New Zealand the Maori people are struggling to gain recognition of their culture and rights. While some Maori resent any of their race being cared for by Pakeha (whites), others are happy for this to occur, providing the rights and cultural needs of the children are respected. We employ Maori and Pacific Island staff and have a policy of working alongside different racial groups. Our cultural programmes are for all residents so that different ethnic groups learn to appreciate each other. Specialised cultural needs are catered for where the resident is willing to follow through with these.

The feminist movement, as well as the pressure by homosexuals and lesbians for recognition of their rights, has brought many challenges to established organisations. One of these is the way men treat women, as sex objects without power. Quite a few young males coming into our Homes have picked up such attitudes, and they are difficult to break down.

The 1985 Staff Training Programme comprised twenty sessions of two and a half hours' duration. These were run in two divisions of ten weeks. The areas covered were: the philosophy of the Trust, including its history; the needs and development of the young (developmental stages, age-appropriate behaviour, implications of impeded development, family and youth fractures, adolescent crises and expectations of the young); and supervision of adolescents (containing out-of-control youth, consultation re proposed interventions in crises, giving and receiving positive and negative feedback, sexual differences, role modelling, psychological and psychiatric problems, parenting and parental involvement).

Also in the Training Programme were sessions on working with families (covering family systems, therapeutic interventions, substitutes for family, staff parental roles and modes of working with separated families); staff needs (caring for one's needs as a staff member, time off, coping with one's own needs and keeping them out of work situations, youth work as a preparation for a career, methods of intercommunication in the work experience); and Special Person assignments (concept of special personning, listening skills, effective confrontation, separation of one's own from others' feelings, awareness of ways in which others' problems activate one's own, distinction between counselling and befriending, recognising transference, contracting, and dealing with sexual attraction in counselling).

Staff were also taught in the programme to deal with special situations such as record keeping, log work, purchasing, advocacy versus taking responsibility for another, community resources, suicide intervention, managing sibling rivalry, dealing with agen-

cies and other organisations, and loyalty to the Trust. The programme also covered particular relationships with residents (coming to terms with exiting processes, rounding off counselling
sessions, planning for life after residential care, aspects of fostering); communication skills (ways of listening, ways of relating to
different ages, socio-economic backgrounds and interpersonal relating); assertiveness (building up personal self-esteem and knowing how to assert oneself); cultural awareness (aspects of Maori
and Island cultures and awareness of these in dealing with youth
and their families); and working under supervision (understanding
the purposes of supervision and how to get the most from the
experience, including self-monitoring).

The remaining sessions were concerned with group facilitation
skills; staff relationships; ways of being creative with others
(methods of involving youth in sporting and leisure activities,
motivating the unmotivated, and ideas for camps, wet weather
experiences and staff shortages); therapeutic and strategic thinking
(reacting to various blocks in working with those in need); evaluation processes (the System Approach, through which change and
progress can be monitored) and other models of youth work (the
final session, dealing with various methods of care, and organisations working with socially and emotionally needy youth).

We have become convinced of the necessity of employing staff
who are mature not only in age but also in emotional development, and have worked through their own problems. But while
staff are important, they are not the only major influence on
young people in care. Peers are a vital factor in determining how
the young behave. Any residential facility which fails to take that
into account, and facilitate positive influence from peers, tends to
find itself in a confrontational rather than a co-operative venture.

Our residential programmes use peer pressure or influence in a
number of ways. Residents are often invited to assist when
another youth is ill, needs overseeing in some consequence for
unacceptable behaviour, needs support in some grief experience,
or requires supervision when out shopping or at a movie. Peers
are often invited to assist, too, when the youth is in trouble and
needs an advocate or help in working through a problem. They
will come to senior staff meetings with a resident or, as happens at
times, if a resident in difficulty runs out of such a meeting, they
will be invited to help him or her to calm down and deal with the
problem.

They are also asked to consider certain behaviours or trends in
the Houses that are proving destructive and to help staff work
toward finding appropriate solutions and strategies. Sometimes,

when there has been a serious offence, residents are left alone to deal with the problem and to find out — without violence, but without staff present — who is responsible for the crime or offensive behaviour. Often they are able to resolve the problem, since they are usually very aware what each other is up to.

The individual resident is also invited as much as possible to be self-determining in his or her behaviour. According to the person's maturity, he or she is encouraged to take on responsibilities in the Houses, such as overseeing work crews, caring for younger residents while they await attention at hospital, or sitting in on some decision-making meetings regarding House policies. The tier or level system in the Houses is one method of structuring this move into taking on responsibility.

The weekly House meetings are important occasions for training residents in confidence and participation in decision-making processes. The appointed resident chairs the meeting, and has to work through an agenda as well as keeping order and ensuring the meeting involves all residents. The chairperson prepares for the meeting beforehand with a senior staff member and learns techniques of control. All new residents are welcomed at such meetings and invited to talk briefly about where they come from and their plans while living in the House.

Something I have often noted, over the years, is the way in which many residents will moan about the fact that there is going to be a meeting, yet seem quite upset if it is cancelled for any reason. It is something they structure their week around, and is also a valuable outlet for their grievances and hurts. On the agenda for any night will be items concerned with stolen clothing, mess in the dining room, swearing, truancy from school, achievements by residents (such as getting a job), matters of information (e.g. a new cook), farewells to departing residents, planning of outings and social activities, and general behaviours that are causing concern.

After sixteen years of attending such meetings (in recent years twice a week, given the two major Houses), one's behind can become very sore from sitting on the floor for a couple of hours as the various items listed on the agenda are worked through. At times I have been very moved by the caring that residents have shown for each other in those settings. I can never be indifferent to such concern. Sometimes the heat of argument is so strong that one wonders whether any successful resolution can be achieved. We try to ensure that the meetings end on a positive note. On occasions when we can get no further with a problem, a smaller group goes on meeting afterwards to achieve some resolution.

Visitors to the Houses over the years have been impressed by the level of honesty and self-revelation that takes place at these gatherings. At times one cringes as all the weaknesses of their communal living are revealed by residents. But the end result is respect for the degree of tolerance and sharing that such meetings show. In my opinion, the House meetings are one of the most vital features in our programme, and help more than most activities to make our communities work.

The weekly House meetings with residents are the main way in which I measure the 'temperature' of the Houses. They give clues about the mood of the House and any tensions that may be building up. They also allow residents to feel they are listened to, besides giving them feedback from their fellows on their ideas. One has to watch that staff do not take over the meetings by talking too much, or merely using the occasion to enforce House rules.

While meetings for residents are important, so is staff communication, as well as sharing with and accepting guidance from people outside the working staff. For this reason I place a high priority on the various times those concerned with the wellbeing of residents and clients get together. Besides regular meetings with officers from the Department of Social Welfare, there are a number of other regular organisational meetings.

Given over thirty staff, the numbers of residents in care and the various segments in the overall project, there is clearly a need for structures to ensure efficient management. The fact that the organisation spends around $900,000 a year, careful accounting and general accountability are required. The Youthlink Trust has developed a number of committees to ensure that the organisation is efficiently run and has points of reference.

At the top of the structure is a group of trustees, who meet bimonthly or more often as business requires, to assess the organisation and to approve new developments. As the project has grown, so has the complexity of the Trustees' work. They comprise a group of people with an interest in young people and with various practical skills relevant to the oversight of such a large operation. The present Trustees are Dr Lindo Ferguson, an eye specialist and former Chancellor of the University of Auckland; Lady Phillipa Tait, a person with wide philanthropic interests; Brian Picot, a founding member of Progressive Enterprises and a company director; and myself, Dr Felix Donnelly, the founder of the Trust and Medical School lecturer. John Graham, an accountant and original helper in setting up the project, is an adviser to the Trustees and attends their meetings.

The Director and Chairman of the Trust are in frequent contact over day-to-day issues, and the various Trustees are members of other management committees within the organisation. Trustees make major decisions concerning expansion moves, buildings, renovations, financial expenditure and funding, and deal with problems affecting the good of the project. An agenda is worked through at each meeting and minutes recorded. A financial statement is circulated and spending projections made. Trustees are also visitors to important functions, such as the opening of new premises or Christmas Day celebrations.

When the Department of Social Welfare provided The Glade, they requested the setting up of a management committee on which they would be represented. This was done, and the Committee has met bimonthly since then. The Management Committee consists of the Chairman and Director of the Trust, the Trustees, the accountant, the administrators of the residential Homes, and senior officers from the Departments of Social Welfare and Justice (Probation). For some years, residents' representatives were present too, and reported back to their fellows at House meetings. However, as sensitive matters came up (e.g. a problem with a staff member, or other confidential issues) it became more difficult for members of the Committee to be able to speak openly. Now the residents' representatives attend on selected occasions, or when they have an issue they want raised.

The Committee oversees the administration of the residential Homes, their financing and their funding. It also offers practical advice and help in getting various enterprises underway — for example, purchasing of land, acquiring a recreation venue, or obtaining a building permit. The Management Committee hears reports from each of the administrators on their Home, looks at proposed expenditure, approves programmes, and assists in the resolution of problems.

In the original setting-up document for this Committee, it was 'to offer practical guidance to the Trust, Director and staff of The Glade in the running of that Home and any other associated projects at the highest level of efficiency and therapeutic effectiveness.' Since then, while encouraging developments and being kept informed about new developments and their ongoing progress, the Committee has restricted itself in management terms to the residential Homes, and separate groups guide other parts of the project.

The original approved document also stated that the Committee 'offers practical management ideas to further the development of the concept of caring effectively for needy youths, and provides practical resources for meeting the needs of the project.' The aims were to gain support and patronage for the Trust, and to ensure continuity in the operation of the Home(s) for needy youth. Now, five years later, that Committee can be assessed as having fulfilled those objectives and making possible the expansion of the work of the Trust.

When the idea of having a school on The Glade site was transformed into a reality, it seemed advisable to have a special Committee to oversee its operation. This was established in 1983; it meets bimonthly, and comprises an Inspector of Special Education, an educational psychologist, a representative from St Peter's College (of which the school is an extension), the teacher(s) of the Glade School, the Glade administrator and the Director of the Trust. These meetings cover the day-to-day running of the school, its practical problems (such as difficult pupils, shortage of materials or staff needs), and improvements. The Committee provides a useful morale boost to the school staff, who often work under difficult circumstances, given the nature of some of the learning problems many of the pupils present. Testing, placement and grading of pupils can be helped through the skills represented on the School Committee. They are also able to inform staff as to what resources are available to them and ways of obtaining these, and they provide a valuable measurement of the quality of work being carried out within the school.

When the project of the Crisis Centre was being developed, it became clear that there was a need for an additional Committee, besides the Management one, to put energy into getting the project off the ground. This was set up and met for two years while negotiations proceeded with the Government. When approval and a promise of financial support were received in late 1984, a new Committee was set up to monitor the work of the Crisis Centre. It now consists of a psychiatrist from the Adolescent Unit, an educational psychologist, a Trustee, a senior member of Youth Aid, a senior officer from the Department of Social Welfare, the Deputy Director and Director of the Trust, and the administrator of the Centre.

They also provide support, advice and comment on the development of this segment of the Trust's work. Every two months they listen to reports on the work of the Crisis Centre and work through an administrative agenda. Their work is similar to that of the Management Committee for the Houses, and provides a similar back-up group to help the Centre function as effectively as possible. The presence of the Leader of the Adolescent Unit, Dr Peter McGeorge, on this Committee provides a link with the work being done with other adolescents in need of special help, and allows for cross referrals between the two agencies.

All the above bodies comprise outside resource people as well as senior members of Youthlink staff, but there are a number of groups that meet regularly within the Trust to ensure good internal communication and planning. The most important of these is the Administrators' Meeting which takes place fortnightly. All the heads of the separate segments of the project meet under the chairmanship of the Director to talk about concerns in each area of work and to settle on policy. Every few months a whole day will be spent sorting out some new development or overcoming an existing problem. This meeting enables each administrator to gain an oversight of the whole operation and share their expertise in problem solving.

The Director also meets individually with the different administrators each week, and so has a composite picture of the entire project. At these meetings, there is no formal agenda. Those looking after the Houses are required to bring up incidents involving criminal or violent behaviour during the past week, though many of these will have already been discussed by administrators with the Director, by phone or on his regular visits to the property during the week.

The group meeting gives the administrators an opportunity to share some of their burdens and gain a sense of support from other senior staff. It promotes co-ordination of resources and a more unified approach to the care of the young. From time to time, the group socialises together in order to improve relationships and avoid a total emphasis on work, thus providing mutual support for each other, and building team spirit.

Other special interest groups in the Trust meet together too. At the therapists' weekly meeting, all those engaged in special therapies with residents, as well as having their individual supervisors, can come together under the chairmanship of the Family Therapist to review individual casework and to learn about strategies for helping young people and their families. This meeting is required for all counsellors who are doing regular sessional work with residents. The Crisis Centre staff are all engaged in such programmes, which tend to be different from those for the residential programmes, so they have their own weekly sessions to meet their particular therapy needs.

Itemising all these major group meetings within the Trust can give an impression of too many meetings or over-management. One of the things we constantly do as an organisation is to review the number and type of meetings we have, since none of us are fans of meetings for the sake of meetings! Those which currently take place are considered by those working in the system to be basic to good functioning, and helpful in maintaining direction. Since I have to attend nearly all these meetings, I sometimes wonder about the need, as I find them crowding in on my calendar. Residents occasionally complain to me about yet another meeting, as they see me hurrying from another engagement to the staff room in their Home. The knowledge of a meeting involving all or some of the staff is like a trigger for these residents to come knocking on the door seeking attention. They also have an insatiable curiosity to know what is going on.

For the internal running of each residential Home, the Crisis Centre and the school, the regular staff meetings are vital. At these, daily events are canvassed, as well as planning ahead. The briefing and debriefing meetings occur twice daily, as one shift ends and the next one begins. Once a week, there is a meeting which the Director attends that goes beyond the daily matters of concern. The feelings and needs of staff are brought out, as well as overall developments and planning. These meetings usually last at least an hour and a half. Any discontents are expected to be raised at such meetings, though sometimes staff prefer to raise their concerns privately, so that they can be brought up during the meeting by someone else.

An annual review of the Trust's objectives reassesses the way things are done, and looks at the structure of management and the groups involved in that process. At times we have tried to cut down on some of the meetings or groups to save time, but inevitably find they are necessary to get the best from staff and maintain accountability. Rather than rush through agendas, it has become evident that people working in an organisation need regular opportunities and leisure to express their concerns. The size and scope of our operation makes these meeting structures necessary, so as to ensure the strength of the Trust.

The meeting that I enjoy most is the one which takes place each week at the residential Homes involving individual residents. The idea is for about twenty to thirty minutes to be spent with a resident, to listen to them and provide some affirmation for them. The selected resident, myself, the House administrator and the relevant Special Person take part. I try to avoid using the time for investigating unsatisfactory behaviour; instead we keep it as a special time to show caring and interest in the young person, review what he or she thinks is happening in their life, and any needs they might have. Frequently the times spent with the resident in that setting can be very revealing. Long-hidden abuses or worries emerge, and some of the sadnesses become apparent. It seems that most of the young people really appreciate this time spent with them by adults who are important to them at that stage of their lives. Whatever good it may do the residents in the Houses, it is an uplifting and renewing experience for me.

PART THREE

Issues in Care

(8)
Being in Care

To some extent we are all 'damaged' during our upbringing. Parents, teachers and those with control over us can make mistakes in dealing with us or situations involving us; they can give messages that permanently undermine self-confidence, or can create insecurities for us. Many of these experiences are softened in their harmful effects by the fact that the child or youth is aware of, and experiences, consistent loving from a parent or two parents. The young person who does not have such bonding is very much at risk, and often lacks the security that tempers ordinary daily life events. Multiple problems can develop as a result.

Marion came into care with the Trust when she was twelve. The story of her life before that was full of problems. She was the child of two people who had had problems in their own childhood. Her father was abandoned when he was twelve, and lived in a series of foster homes. Marion's mother, who came from a broken home, had been taken into the care of the State when she was fourteen. She was said to be promiscuous and out of control. Those who dealt with her in her teen years commented that she had a very low sense of self-worth. This had been intensified by beatings from her father and by being expelled from school several times.

She had married at eighteen, and was pregnant at the time. After the birth of a son, she suffered from depression and had several spells in a psychiatric hospital. Neighbours complained to the police about the frequent screams from the home, as they realised the mother was beating her two young children. Marion at this stage was fourteen months old. In court Marion's mother admitted frequently beating her children; she said she had an uncontrollable temper and suffered from severe depression. Marion was found to have sores on her body, and her buttocks were lacerated.

The children were taken out of the mother's care (the father had left home) and initially they were kept together in a foster home, but when Marion was two and a half, they were separated. For the next ten years Marion's life consisted of many different homes. Fostering arrangements broke down because her behaviour became extremely difficult for people to manage. She was a consistent bed-wetter, as well as daily wetting her pants. She also constantly stole from home and neighbours, and anyone who befriended her was at risk, as she would burgle their home. No efforts to stop either the enuresis or thieving were successful.

When Marion was ten, an attempt was made to reunite her with her mother. This proved disastrous, as the man then living with her mother was a sadist, and on several occasions hung Marion up by straps and beat her, as well as sexually interfering with her. So it was back to care once again. Many of those who tried to foster Marion believed their own marriage was at risk because of the pressures her presence in the family placed on their relationship. The inability of medical resources to overcome the wetting problem caused any attempts at adoption to collapse too.

Marion was seen by a series of child psychologists and then psychiatrists, as people tried to effect changes in her behaviour. Her temper tantrums and abuse of authority figures were further grounds for concern. It was becoming impossible to find any home that would accept her for fostering. Eventually she was placed in a children's psychiatric ward; her behaviour was observed, and programmes to modify it were set up. Staff reported that she was something of a menace in the ward — screaming at staff, stealing from them, and continuing her lack of bladder control. When interviewed, Marion would not look people in the eye, but would turn her head away and often weep, though seeming to be angry that she showed those feelings. Any attempts to comfort her were pushed aside angrily.

On one occasion, Marion got hold of some black dye and poured it over hospital notes, carpet and uniforms. As usual when confronted with such behaviour, she denied it. The medical team felt Marion had little control over her emotions. Her mood swings were sudden and inexplicable. She began to try to get close to staff, clearly seeking affection: the more that was given, the more seemed to be needed. She now began stealing other children's clothing, especially underwear, since hers was constantly wet. She would hide her pants in all sorts of places — the back of drawers and cupboards, or in trees and bushes.

The enuretic problem meant that Marion at times smelt, and she was subject to a lot of teasing from other children. She became isolated and lonely. To win friends, Marion shared the spoils of her thieving excursions. Any improvements in her behaviour were short-lived, as Marion would return to the old patterns of lying and stealing. Various interventions were attempted to change her wetting behaviour. Gold stars were placed on a card when she remembered to go regularly to the toilet, and she was made to wash her own soiled underwear, as well as shower whenever she wet her pants.

As she got older, Marion became more aggressive and rude toward those helping her. She also tended to bully younger children. She was eventually discharged from hospital, as it was felt little permanent progress was being made, and she was a severe drain on staff resources. She was placed in a children's home, and the usual patterns of behaviour continued.

It was at this point that we were invited to take Marion in as a referral. The nursing staff and chief psychiatrist at the hospital gave us a full briefing on the girl's past history and problems. Planning meetings were held, and yet another group became involved in the long history of changing faces in Marion's life.

It was suggested that the origins of this girl's wetting problems went back to her early toilet training, when she was spanked for soiling her pants. The theory was that she held on to the point of soiling, and eventually passed that critical age where one should have learnt to heed the warnings that the bladder needed emptying. This meant she was unable to hold on or take appropriate action when urination was required.

It was clear to the staff at The Glade that Marion was in need of a stable and caring environment, with close supervision. It had originally seemed that the best environment for Marion would be a small family group, but we, and those responsible for her, had been unable to find such a placement. From talking with some of the people who had been concerned in the various stages of Marion's life, I became aware that many people had been involved, including medical professionals, in trying various strategies to change the young girl's behaviour. All of them had started off with initial hope that they would succeed where others had failed. My own optimism with her rose and fell as event followed event.

There were the good times, when this intelligent girl received good academic reports from school, or was especially friendly and co-operative. Then, suddenly and apparently inexplicably, the police would return her to the Home; or we would notice that she had some expensive piece of equipment; or rotting, smelling, ruined underwear would be discovered; or abuse and rejection would come to all the staff. In spite of all these factors, Marion stayed longer with us than with any other home, and made a number of important steps forward.

We had tried to encourage contact with her mother, who lived several hundred miles from Auckland. What we soon learnt, however, was that her trips home always ended in some disaster or deep upset for Marion. At times her mother would not see her, after her travelling down to visit. On one occasion the mother called the police to order her out. This was one of the deepest hurts the girl experienced. It then dawned on her, at fourteen years of age, that there was little future in that relationship, at least at that stage.

Marion initially reacted to the rejection by thieving, abusive behaviour toward us, and damage to her mother's property. When she calmed down, she commented that she would have to stop trying to make further contact with her mother until she was older and could handle the mother's reactions.

Over the years we, like those before us, tried all kinds of ways of helping Marion stop her wetting patterns. As she got older, she became more motivated to stop her problem herself. She began to take more pride in herself, and this made her co-operative in following regimes established to change her behaviour. She also bonded very strongly with a mature female staff member, who took the time to follow up consistently any wetting or stealing incidents that occurred. She would take Marion back to school when she ran away because of soiling, and made her clean her own sheets and underwear.

This accountability helped modify, though not completely re-move, many of Marion's undesirable actions. When other staff and I talked with the young girl in moments of relaxation, she would sometimes share her desperate need to belong. She wanted whichever staff member who was close to her to adopt her. Her thoughts were so often of her mother, and her anger was mostly against those of us she thought were barriers to her going back. She really did not want to face the fact that she was not important to her mother, or had little place in her life.

Her enuretic problem was more pronounced under stress, so we tried to teach her regular elimination habits and stress reduc-tion techniques. To some extent these were helpful in lessening the behaviours and improving her social skills. It was also observ-able that the girl's periods of happiness, with less moodiness, were more frequent than previously, and the security she experienced had helped improve her self-esteem.

Marion's story has been repeated in the lives of many young people who have come into our care over the last decade and a half. The early crippling damage can never be totally overcome, but it is possible to help such a person gain coping skills that offer the possibility of some quality of life. Marion was not helped only by coming to us. There have been many caring people over the years — foster parents, social workers, professionals — who have shown her respect and care, and have cumulatively helped her to respond positively to some of the support offered her. But for Marion, and many other Marions, the hunger for acceptance by a parent goes on, and those working with youngsters in care need to accept and appreciate that primary yearning.

Young people in care often complain of things they had to endure in homes or state-run institutions. A 'Speak Out Camp' for young people living away from their families was held in New South Wales, Australia, in 1979. What follows are some of the statements made by the participants at that Camp, and recorded by the organisers (NSW Association of Child Caring Agencies) who shared them with me.

They treat you as a Group, not an Individual.

There's too much of a timetable. It's just like a dead person, you come home, you do this, you do that.

A place with so many kids — you need rules, but in some places there's too many rules — you just can't live by them. I think a good rule comes from the kids themselves. Our freedom comes from us as well as them.

The thing that gets me is that if I tell the staff the truth, I get into more trouble than if I tell them a lie. So you might as well tell them lies. And everyone says, if you tell the truth, then you get into a lot less trouble. It's a lotta bull.

I was getting worried, I was that down. It wasn't funny, no-one would talk to me. All they do is give you lectures, all the time. Sometimes you just don't want lectures — just some-one to talk to!

Oh it's just mainly the boys that get punishment.

Sometimes I feel as if I am owned by the State.

The only thing you see of your file is when they've got it out and you're standing around and having a peek.

The kids don't have a say. They just get picked up and put down. Picked up and put down.

There should be proper standard rules you know and every kid shown them when they first come to the home.

Kids in care you know, they don't know what their position is, like where they are. Like they don't know what the mana-ger's rights are, you know, what he can do and what he can't and that sort of thing. We should be let in on that I reckon.

Most people think that if you're in homes, then you're a cri-minal or something. That's what they think 'homes' means.

You need one permanent person.

We've had four sets of house parents in two years.

I'm scared of leaving and going out on my own. I'm scared they'll throw me out.

To balance these negative reactions, here are some of the more positive comments from young people in care:

When I go on holidays I miss the home — I always want to go back.

People ask you crazy questions — they just don't realise that it's like a normal home.

We just tell the matron 'cause we class her as our mother. If we've got a problem we'll go to her and talk about it to her. It's easy to talk to her.

Having kids come to tea is really important to me, because it's just like a home then.

It's really good at the home because they treat me like a normal kid. . . . I get into trouble like anyone else.

We can send our letters and no one will read them.

It was scary the first time and then I got used to it.

We've got plenty of freedom at our place. It just depends on your behaviour.

It's really good the way they trust us.

I like the way in which we have a say in what we do and what happens.

But for every positive comment, there were twenty negative ones from the youngsters. I have attended foster care gatherings in Australia and New Zealand, where representatives of youth who have been in care have spoken with considerable anger against some of their experiences in homes. What emerges is a resentment that they had so many placements, especially during their teen years, that there were so many changes of social workers appointed to look after them, that they had little say in what happened to them, that the staff often broke the rules to suit themselves, and that they had a label of being different, because they were in care.

The research into characteristics of children in residential care, and our own experiences in Youthlink, identify a number of factors. One of these is that the youngster who has had broken relationships or negative ones during early childhood, will tend to perceive all adults with suspicion, but will respond initially to any friendly approaches of staff with anger. Since the young person has been taken away from their family home, there is a vital need for the child to form a real adult relationship. This has to be a

120

one-to-one relationship, with emotion and affection being expressed within it on the part of the youngster and the adult. It is equally important that this relationship have some intensity about it, as well as continuity.

Children who have been some time in residential care are often unmotivated and want others, particularly their carers, to do things for them. They often feel the State should provide for them, even though they could be self-reliant. This attitude carries over to their clothing and others' property, for which they often have little respect. They believe these things can be easily replaced.

The young in care need to have around them people who are vital, rather than cynical, tired or worn out. Staff with no enthusiasm and energy are not suited to caring for young people. Similarly, those who engage in therapy with them need to have some personal dynamism and be able to get alongside them. This means the young person sees the therapist as understanding what is being expressed or felt, not pushy or judgemental, and respectful of the youth and his or her rights. This takes time and patience to achieve.

Studies also reveal that disturbed and misbehaving youth are usually reacting to social and environmental factors. They are reacting to external pressures. When the environment is changed to one that includes caring from mature adults, and interaction with suitable people around their own age, they usually gradually change their behaviour and develop acceptable ways of coping with their frustrations.

Group living for young people offers socialising opportunities for them which build their confidence. The adults working with them need to watch over the criticisms that can come from their peers, but also encourage mutual support. The common needs and problems experienced by these young people help create such a supportive environment, and allow for involving the group in problem-solving. It has been found to be necessary for youth living in homes to have opportunities for times of solitude and privacy. So residential homes need to provide quiet areas and allow the residents to have time on their own, or time-out away from the home or institution.

The experience for young persons of living away from their families does not have to be a negative one, or always a second best placement. For it to be successful and heal some of the hurts that deprivation brings, the voices of those who live in care need to be listened to, and the staff need to be sensitive to their needs and developmental processes.

Yet those who work in foster care areas or in residential homes for young people often feel criticised or unappreciated in the difficult task they carry out. The ideal would be for every youngster to be kept in his or her own home. But there are cases where this is impossible, if there is to be any care for the youngster or the family. Perhaps most criticism is levelled at those places that take in numbers of young persons in need.

There are a number of 'dirty words' in child care work and among many social workers. One of these has become the term 'institution'. There is a concerned effort — and it is a commendable one — to 'keep young people out of institutions'. What makes a place an institution is not usually clear. All my life I have tried to make the Homes I have been concerned with non-institutional. But as the project has grown, and as more and more young people and their families have pleaded with me for accommodation and acceptance, I have felt obliged to extend the size of the Homes offering care.

I object to the blanket labelling of places as 'institutional' in a pejorative sense, because of their size. It seems to me that what really makes an 'institution' has little to do with numbers, and much to do with its mode of operation. The 'institutions' that I would like to try and keep the young out of are those that are primarily in existence to contain difficult or criminal young people, that stigmatise them, that allow them little say in their own destiny, that are not involved in therapeutic endeavours clearly good for their inhabitants, that do not allow the growth of self-esteem, that ignore individual differences and social and emotional needs; places where the needs of the organisation take priority over the needs of the individual.

Some remand homes, schools, hospitals and family homes are aptly described in those institutional terms. But other so-called 'institutions' do not operate in such ways. They are therapeutic, in that they create an environment that is conducive to positive change, within which individuals experience respect and are consulted about what happens to them. They offer programmes suitable to their users' needs, and these are evaluated and changed so that they are achieving what they were planned to accomplish. These places also ensure that there is harmony between the needs of the institution or its environment, and the needs of its residents, and work on erasing the conflicts.

Over the time I have worked in youth care, it has been possible for me to experiment with many variables. I have worked in houses of every size, with no structured programme through to extensive programming, where residents have scant say in their destiny or are always consulted about those items of concern to them. It has become clear, through experimenting, reading and visiting other similar projects, that the most successful and youth-related set-ups are those that have the following qualities: they enhance individual self-worth, are non-confrontational in their approach, work out their clients' needs and endeavour to meet these. They have a reasonable structure that residents understand, help to create, and that is consistent and fair. They consult residents in all decision-making processes concerning them, do not engage in labelling residents, and involve as far as possible the client's family or quasi-family. They require accountability for behaviour, respond systematically to positive as opposed to negative behaviour, and encourage independent, as distinct from dependent, living.

There are some youngsters who do not succeed in a large living complex. For some, even three people are too many to handle. They will normally not do well in an environment with other young people. But there are a very large number of young people today who long for the chance of living and mixing with lots of other young people around their own age. In such a setting, they can develop skills in mixing with others, overcome self-centred behaviours that normally isolate them, and experience healthy pressure from their peers to conform in areas where conformity is essential.

Most of the weddings I perform as a priest are for the young people who have lived in my care. Many of them are not Catholics, but wish me to join them on this important occasion. It is always a personal joy for me to do so. Often I have not seen them for some years after their leaving one of our Homes. We have had a few weddings at The Glade, and these have been eagerly watched by present residents. Not very long ago, I assisted at the wedding of a girl in her mid-twenties. She was radiantly happy on her wedding day, and her choice of partner seemed a good one. I do not on such occasions refer to the hostel days in any specific way, because for many, those were times of struggle and great personal emotion. But my mind turns back to those days, and runs almost on two tracks as I recollect the past.

Maria was a reluctant starter at our Home. She came to the admission interview rebellious and unco-operative. Her social worker was patient and slightly desperate. The truth was that no one wanted Maria. She had been through eighteen foster placements in two years, and they had all broken down. The girl claimed that in most cases she had not been told why she should leave the place which was meant to be her home. It was clear that there was nowhere else for the girl to go, but she seemed totally uninterested in what was about to happen to her, and switched off what was going on around her. So the interview ended up mainly a conversation between the social worker and the two of us from Youthlink. We agreed to accept Maria and to give her three weeks to make up her mind whether she wished to be a part of us. She turned her head away and gave no indication whether this was what she wanted. As the social worker was leaving, she muttered 'I won't stay, you know. I will run away and nobody will stop me!' She did run away, within ten minutes of her statement. But after a scary night out in a park, she came back the following morning, creeping into the room assigned to her. Slowly, she became caught up in the life of the House.

I was later to find out a number of significant factors in her life. She deeply resented her parents disowning her (she was adopted, and they had long since felt they could not cope with her stealing from them and her lies). She felt that she was less loved than the other 'natural' children in the family. There was incredible bitterness toward her mother, and anger that she had been fostered out. (At that stage Maria was unwilling to acknowledge any problems she may have presented for her family.)

In every foster home she went to, she resented the foster parents' children, because she felt they had security and belonged, while she didn't. She continued her history of lies and theft, and found the fuse of most of those taking her in was quite short. So she moved from placement to placement, and in the process had several different social workers allotted to her, as they left for other employment or received promotion. Maria was clear, when she eventually filled in our assessment form, that she had no friends and that nobody really cared about her. At that stage she was saying that she didn't want any friends, because she did not trust anybody.

She quickly set about getting herself removed from the House. She stole from the other girls in the bedroom, especially their underwear and make-up. At first, Maria would not take part in House jobs or outings. She was used to being a loner, and wanted to continue in that role, and she soon asked me for a bedroom on her own. I pointed out why that would not be a good thing, given her socialising problems, even had we such rooms to spare. Her Special Person complained to us about the difficulties in trying to communicate with Maria. She would not talk, and the worker found herself answering her own questions. It was difficult not to start yawning, or even to stay awake, in the course of some of her sessions with Maria.

The breakthrough came gradually, as it usually does in such cases, and it was not from what we as staff were doing. Another girl was admitted into the House who was slightly handicapped, and was rather terrified of the numbers at first. Maria felt drawn to her in her obvious discomfort, and began acting as her protector and confidant. This opening out to one person gradually spread to others in the House, including several males. These thirty-five other young people were in a similar position to herself; Maria came to find them unthreatening (compared to the children belonging to foster parents) and slowly began to assert herself. There were other features in her gradual change, such as improving her self-image, modifying her stealing patterns, and returning to school at eighteen to get her University Entrance Examination. The blossoming out came over two years, as the angry, shy and unlikeable girl gained confidence, overcame her lying and thieving and, what for her ultimately was the most important change, felt accepted back into her family.

Three years' living with us was a long time out of her life, and when she eventually went flatting she talked about what had been important for her in moving into our House. She said that above all else, it was the experience of having to mix with so many other people who were in situations not unlike her own, many of them even worse off. She felt that there was such a wide range of different types to associate with that she was able to find people with whom she could form friendships. She had also appreciated that at times the spotlight was off her because of the numbers, and she was able to enjoy others having attention focused on them, especially for behaviour for which she had always been the centre of attraction. Maria got a lot out of her stay with us, and gave a good deal back before she moved on to the next step in her life. It was the variety of young people that was a powerful factor in bringing about a willingness to change and reshape her self-image.

In today's world, where much of the excitement has gone out of family life because of parental busyness, electronic media dominance, and small family groupings, many youth are searching at adolescence for a chance to live with people their own age. It is not fair to condemn any experiences offered to the young that help them meet these needs in a supervised and secure way. The movement of youngsters onto the streets has in part been a search for this sense of belonging and acceptance by their peers. We do not understand young people if we do not acknowledge their strong need to socialise and share with their own age group. Those who have been deprived of normal parental closeness have a deep need to experience the independence and acceptance which close living with their peers can bring. I believe our experiences with thousands of youngsters over many years have clearly shown that there are a significant number of young people who have benefited from living with a large number of their peers, because of their special needs at that point in their life.

The struggle for all those who run hostels which offer more than beds and food is to make sure they do not lose their heart and become sterile, rule-bound places, that choke the individuality and freedom of youth. It is a constant struggle to prevent the institutional needs swallowing up the personal ones. Always the consumers' needs have to be kept paramount in running such places.

Some who came to work in Youthlink during its pioneer days have had to struggle with the problems and changes that growth has brought. The greater demands on effective communication that bigger staff numbers bring about, and the amount of time spent in training and sharing, bring back nostalgic memories of less systematic times, where paperwork and consultation had a lower priority. It is understandable that worries surface about whether the earlier, more family-like model is suffering.

What we have come to face is that you can have, and in fact must have, consistency, clarity of decision-making, planned programmes and a workable structure if you are to achieve worthwhile developments for residents. But it is vital that the possible formality and coldness of processes do not predominate in the project. That means the qualities that make for good family life, such as unity among the parents, respect for one another irrespective of age or position, caring attitudes, affirmation of each other, recognition of effort, and good communication opportunities all operate in the organisation. Institutions do not have to be cold and destructive of personal identity. When the system is controlled by people who do care about each other, are open and warm, and are aware of the vulnerability of those in care, they can make the necessary institutional structures therapeutic, and a framework for great personal growth and caring.

(9)
Racial Concerns

At the present time, New Zealand is undergoing an intense and growing examination of where it stands on racial issues. Our society has been accused of fostering racism, and the finger has been pointed at institutions such as the Justice, Education, Health and Social Welfare Departments. The strong complaint is that the Pakeha have used power to undermine and make dependent the Maori people, who claim to be the tangata whenua, deprived of their rightful heritage. The Maori would point to the disproportionate numbers of their people to be found in penal institutions, mental hospitals, the courts, welfare institutions, and among the unemployed, as evidence of this racism.

They are asking for the resources and power to deal with their own needs and people in a manner that is in accord with their cultural values and meets their spiritual needs. They believe a century and a half of white domination has left them undermined and with a fight on their hands to preserve their culture, in particular their language and lands. They go further than just stating that they want the freedom and means to develop their culture; many claim that the values of Pakeha society are dangerous to the spirit and the wellbeing of the Maori as a people.

As an institution that has increasingly been involved with needy Maori youth, Youthlink has had to address the problems that the new Maori renaissance has highlighted. At any given time, the number of Maori youngsters in our homes would be close to 50 percent of all residents. While there have never been apparent divisions among residents on a racial basis, and Maori, Pacific Islanders and Pakehas have blended in well, as young people are able to do, they are aware of the conflict out in the wider community. Very rarely it will surface in a moment of intense anger, when a Maori youth might call a female staff member 'a white honky'. But these are the exceptions.

At times in the past few years, we have had some outsiders expressing anger at Maori youth being in a Pakeha institution. Some residents have told us that they have been berated for living where they do. On one occasion, some older Maori spoke strongly to a sixteen-year-old Maori male about his being at The Glade. He came back to us with a lot of resentment and anger. From that point on, it became almost impossible to deal with him. He became violent, smashing in doors, windows and other items of value. We got the elders in to talk to him and encourage him to fit in. They explained what they had meant, which they said was not so much a criticism of The Glade, but of his lack of identifying with things Maori. Even that did not work. The resentment at cultural deprivation can be extremely strong.

On another occasion a Maori boy who had been doing a lot of thieving was taken from our care, without consultation, by a youngish Maori court worker. She told him that he should be back with his parents, and put him onto transport to return to his home, which was well out of Auckland. We had been working to get him home, but a lot of reconciliation had to be done with the neighbours in his home town, from whom he had stolen a great deal of property. He lasted two days back home before he was driven out by local hostility and his response to that. He ended up back on the streets, sniffing glue.

I wrote to those responsible for the court worker, but got no reply. This highlights the difficulties that surround issues of this kind, and white authorities are becoming loath to get involved in such situations. Some would argue that in the case of this Maori boy, he was better off even on the streets, which he made his home, than in a Pakeha environment. They would feel the need for the boy to identify with his own people is a greater good than keeping out of crime or off the streets.

We have had to handle similar situations on occasions, and have been careful not to battle against the basic principle that a Maori child should be with his or her own people, if they have the resources and commitment to care for that young person. Sometimes the family concerned have overridden a Maori social worker's wish to remove the child from one of our homes, and have insisted that their child remain in our care.

Since we have heightened our awareness of Maori issues and needs in recent times, and made greater contact with the Maori community, there have not been any repeats of the type of episode described above. But we are conscious that these issues require delicate management, and are to be expected at a time of considerable tension between Maori and Pakeha over some issues.

Over the greater part of the Trust's history, the presence of Maori and Pacific Island residents was taken for granted, and the cultural needs were addressed as was thought appropriate. In earlier times, quite a number of Maori youth did not want to put much energy into learning their own culture, since it appeared to have a low value in the general society in which they moved. We have often made attempts to involve Maori youth in marae visits, and have tried to set up opportunities for their cultural values to be developed within the Homes. But it is only within the last three years that we have gone out of our way to emphasise strongly the Maori and Pacific Island contacts with their own people.

This came to a head early in 1986, when we had a staff day that addressed racism and our own contribution to it. At this study day only the Pakeha staff were present, helped by two facilitators who have done a good deal of work in this area. Out of that day came a lot of soul-searching and consciousness-raising about the dislocation of Maori people that had occurred since the coming of Europeans to this country. We acknowledged the ways in which the law, resources, behaviours and values that dominated society bore scant relation to the rights and needs of Maori people. It was made clear that because of a long history of Maori people being asked to advise Pakehas, and this advice then not being followed, there now exists scant trust of Pakehas and an unwillingness for Maori to tell the whites what to do to rectify the situation. It was also established that a Pakeha will never have a complete understanding of Maori culture, since there will be some things never disclosed, in order for the Maori to retain an identity.

Among the findings made by the staff that study day were that the Maori were a disadvantaged and oppressed people. Many of them hate Pakeha society as it now exists, with so much stress placed on material wealth. Yet the Maori are saying that their people want an equal share in society and in its exercise of power. It was noted that many Maori young people have felt, 'I am a Maori — everything that is bad about me is because I'm a Maori.' It was also clear that many Maori had a different idea of family and extended family from the Pakeha. Maori also wish to determine those issues that directly affect them. The Maori people are saying that things have not worked well for them under the present system, so they should be given a chance to change things to their way of living and thinking.

What seems to be a major thrust of Maoridom today is to be self-determining. For this to happen, the Pakeha has to face that our country is mostly monocultural in the way it operates. As an organisation directly affecting some Maori youth and families, Youthlink is trying to address issues of racism. At the seminar we had felt that there was a lack of understanding of Maori needs in the young, that ours was mainly a Pakeha system run by Pakehas, and that most of the Pacific Island and Maori residents who come to us have lost their cultural identity, and have little security as a result.

Some felt that we tended to spoil young Maori, not making

them sufficiently self-reliant and allowing them to speak to adults (elders) in a way that would not be tolerated in a Maori setting. In this way, they were not learning respect. It was also stated that many Maori people are envious of the resources that Youthlink has and would like them for themselves.

We looked at what our approach to these issues was at that point. It was clear we were concerned; this concern had culminated in the seminar, and was shown by the further time spent on racism at later seminars. While we already employed some Maori and Pacific Island staff, it was decided to raise their numbers. We thought it would be a good idea to set up a Maori Advisory Group as part of the Trust. It would be able to assist us in gaining sensitivity to Maori issues. While there had been some attempt to locate resources in the community relevant to Maori residents, this needed to be increased.

It was also pointed out that we were represented on a committee working for improved Maori, Pacific Island and Pakeha residential facilities for youth (Te Whakakaianga), and had made efforts to support Maori endeavours through that body. We had run a Wananga on Parenting that brought various ethnic groups, especially Maori, together over a weekend. The Crisis Centre had also been involved in supporting networks in the community dealing with Maori youth.

However, we acknowledged that these efforts had been piecemeal and sporadic. There was no consensus-based organisational response evident. There was a clear will from the staff to change and improve our biculturalism, but some confusion as to what direction we should take. Some wondered whether there was sufficient will to change in the organisation. The concern overall was how we could meet the needs of children from varied cultural backgrounds.

Like most Pakeha groups who take the journey into examining their racism, the experience was painful, at times moving, and brought new awareness of the problems of which we were a part. We had originally met without Maori staff present, since the 'oppressed' ought not to be a part of the 'oppressors' examining their consciences. Later we invited the Maori members of staff to be observers at discussions on the remedies we proposed taking.

We tried to set up a Maori Advisory Group to assist our Trust in maintaining an awareness of racial issues, appropriate dealing with Maori residents, and improved contacts with their whanau (family), and to help in employing Maori staff and developing cultural programmes within the Homes. We held several meetings to this end, and invited some Maori who worked with young people to join us. What immediately became clear was that an 'advisory group' was an inappropriate response. The Maori people had grown tired of being 'advisors' to Pakehas. It was pointed out to us that if we could not do the job properly for Maori youth, then we should hand over our resources to the Maori people.

Those who came to the meetings challenged us to share our power and resources with the Maori people. They also turned us toward our own Maori staff, urging us to listen to them and make sure they were an integrated part of our organisation. When we listened to our Maori staff, we heard them saying that they wanted us to work alongside them, not separately from the Maori people. So that pointed us in a direction that we have since followed.

On our Administrative Committee we have a senior Maori staff member, in addition to any other Maori who might hold administrative office (at present the Administrator of the Family Home and Rowan House). We have also increased the number of Maori employed by the Trust to over a third of all staff. We have tried to appoint some of these to senior positions, and to have special responsibility for Maori children in our care. We are continuing, as opportunity arises, to appoint more Maori staff and give them positions of power and responsibility within the Trust.

While there is a hierarchical structure in our organisation, we have tried to follow the Maori approach of more open discussion among staff, with a freedom for all to speak their mind. We have increased the number of marae visits for all our residents. Maori leaders and speakers have also regularly visited and spoken to our residents.

Before admitting a Maori child to our Homes through the Crisis Centre, we involve our Maori social worker and she checks with the youth's whanau whether this placement meets their wishes and is in the best interests of the child. The family are invited to maintain contact with us, and are made welcome to visit. In the care of Maori youth, we often consult with Maori healers and at times with their spiritual leaders. We try to get our Maori staff to work on spiritual issues with the Maori residents.

We have also set up Maori language and cultural programmes for residents. These began as classes three days a week at the Glade School, but were later extended to the Crisis Centre, where a Maori staff member runs a weekly three-hour programme, attended by many residents and some staff. There are regular cultural evenings run for working residents at Rowan House. Most residents enjoy these gatherings and respond positively in their behaviour outside the sessions. They use the Maori language more, observe etiquette requirements special to Maori people, and gain self-respect, as well as more courtesy for their elders.

Recently we held a presentation of awards following sporting achievements. This gathering at The Glade was the best attended gathering of parents we have ever had. A special feature of it was the large number of Maori parents who attended. Pleasing, too, were the achievements of so many of the Maori youth in attaining awards. Their pride in achievement was evident.

Another area of racial need that we have only recently begun to address is that of food or diet. Maori food has not featured to any degree in our meal planning. We have had hangis, proudly prepared by Maori residents, on many occasions, but have not made a point of including special Maori foods in the diet. Now that our attention has been drawn to the importance of this, the residents participate in going out into country areas to gather items such as puha and watercress. Once or twice a week, the main meal consists of Maori food (pork bones, muttonbirds, fish and so on) prepared by Maori staff assisted by residents.

The issue of separatism is still very much alive. The debate about whether separate homes should exist for Maori children in care goes on. There are such places already in existence, and these often include Pakeha residents. Those who support separatist development usually see it as a necessary transitional stage, consistent with self-determination for the Maori people. The claim is that Taha Maori can only be achieved by having a home run completely on Maori values, culture and language.

In Youthlink we are treading our way with sensitivity, and endeavouring to be open to what seems best for the care of the young. Patience, understanding and time are all part of making the best decisions on the question of racism. Our Trust is aware of longstanding societal neglect of Maori needs. The answers are still being argued and sought. Youthlink has made a commitment to that quest, and is trying to address the problem as carefully as possible. This means a constant need to be open to criticism, and to re-examine our position.

If we ask the residents what they want in terms of living in a totally Maori or bicultural setting, the answers are mixed. Some have tried living in a totally Maori environment; it has not suited them, and they have walked away from it. Others have gone from a setting like ours and found their needs better met in a Maori setting. At present, I think there is a place for all kinds of homes. Not every residential home run by Maori is necessarily fully Maori in its orientation. Some Maori people (and this reflects the problem the Maori people are addressing) have little appreciation of what their culture is about, and have not yet come to terms with being Maori.

This dilemma was brought out in our staff seminar on racism. A younger member who had a fairly brown skin had claimed not to be a Maori, even though of Maori parentage. At the second seminar on racism, where Maori staff present spoke of their hurts and what being Maori meant to them, he visibly changed. In a dramatic speech near the end of the day, this young man cried as he spoke of having turned his back on his culture and why he had done this, in order to identify fully with the dominant white society. Since then he has attended the Maori language and cultural classes we run, seeking to identify with his own people.

Many of our residents are like that young staff member; they have had little exposure to authentic Maori tradition and values in their rearing, so they tend to have some resistance to taking up the study of their language and culture. Usually this is only an initial reluctance, and soon gives way to curiosity and interest. We have seen shy, very quiet Maori youngsters come out of their shells when on a marae, participating with confidence in Maori songs, stick games and action dances.

There are difficulties in sustaining the efforts we are making to be bicultural. It takes energy and commitment; sometimes the willingness is there on our part, but we are unable to get help from the Maori community or the plans made break down. Nevertheless, we believe that if we are to help fully the Maori youth in our care, we must address their cultural heritage and encourage the efforts made to envelop them in it.

We have Maori crafts taught at our Homes, and carving in bone or wood is popular. We are setting up a small marae at The Glade, which residents are now working on, contributing carvings and paintings and general decoration. When completed, this will be our base for all cultural programmes, for special meetings, and as a quiet place for our staff and residents. It is a step in a movement toward helping Maori youth, families and staff to feel at home in the Youthlink environment.

(10)
Stresses and Rewards

There are many stresses involved in the care of socially and emotionally needy adolescents. Most of these come from within the
job itself, such as violent behaviour, runaways, criminal acts by
some residents, or drug overdosing. They are expected problems
within the job. What is more difficult to deal with are the criticisms from outside. Anyone working in youth care must have
experienced the jealousies and destructive put-downs of those
outside, who are quick to spring to judgement and unwilling to
find out the other side of the story.

As Director, I write at least one letter a week correcting mis-
information regarding something our organisation is supposed to
have done or not done. A letter arrives criticising the fact that a
girl arriving for the holidays in another part of the country, had
only the clothes she stood up in. Then there is an official complaint over the lack of clothing we were providing. No check was
first made with us as to what the girl left our home with. In fact
she sold her clothes for extra pocket money, between leaving the
hostel and arriving home. Fortunately, some families and agencies
are well aware of the many possibilities that can change the basis
for criticism, and they check things out first.

This is not to say that we have not made mistakes in our work
with youth. Stress and a shortage of resources can make for mis-
taken management from time to time. In addition, expectations of
individuals and communities can and do change. One has to note
changing needs, such as the need for residential care for younger
children, and respond accordingly. Over thirty years of this work,
I have learnt to listen carefully and with an open mind to all sides
of a story. Disturbed youngsters can at times imagine as real
things that are part of their fantasy life — for example, an imagined
sexual assault that in fact never happened, when an affectionate
hug can be thought back on as a sexual advance. These misunderstandings make for difficulty for the residential worker, and therefore require staff to be very careful about protecting themselves.

In listening to two or more sides of an accusation against a
resident or a staff member, there are inevitably distortions, usually
unintentional, that show the preoccupation of the narrator, and
sometimes their biases. Misunderstandings, especially reading particular motives into actions, are commonplace. Residential workers are very vulnerable to criticism and accusations from people

they displease. It is always hurtful to hear about false accusations being made by some embittered former resident who had left angry or had done little to help themselves. One can spend many hours tracing such stories and trying to set the record straight.

Others running similar projects all relate stories of complaints like these, and the problems they can generate. The difficulty is repairing some of the damage to one's good name, particularly where people or agencies are only too willing to believe the worst. However, there are many others who value the work which organisations such as Youthlink undertake, and who understand the thanklessness of much of the work, and the very limited resources available to carry out what are extremely demanding tasks.

Critical feedback is essential if any organisation is to grow and achieve its purposes. It is also vital that groups working with vulnerable young people are accountable, and are constantly working toward an ideal operation. But it can be hard to cope with criticism, no matter how valid, when workers are under siege through the heavy workload they carry, and the emotional demands it makes. Our work with youth owes a great deal to those who have been able to comment both critically and appreciatively about what we are doing, and have been supportive in assisting us to respond to criticism.

It is the live-in staff who usually face the greatest pressures; it is essential that they have appreciation, support, and time-out to cope with the constant battery of demands on them. Those who carry administrative responsibility for keeping their unit functioning at top level, meeting the demands of staff, residents, and people like myself, and ensuring that our procedures are followed, are under severe pressure. When someone is constantly surrounded by young people with problems, in great need of attention, and often resenting any authority figure, it requires rare qualities to remain calm, never shout at people, and never show impatience or exhaustion.

Dilemmas arise in some management situations. For example, we have a policy of notifying the local police of any criminal behaviour by a resident. This can rebound against us. Some police become annoyed about being involved in small thefts such as a packet of cigarettes. We can also get a name for harbouring criminals, given the number of times we are in touch with the police. The neighbours may resent seeing police cars at our Homes, and this may add fuel to their fears about the places being full of criminals.

Other problems arise over our own policies; we can find put-

135

ting them into effect very difficult. We assure our neighbours, for their protection, that any resident who seriously affronts them will be dismissed from the House. Suppose a couple of youths offend a nearby neighbour; one of them has been doing very well with us, but we are required to ask him to leave because of our policy. Or a resident threatens a particular staff member with physical violence, and sometimes it ends up as a case of 'either he goes or I go'. These issues require careful negotiation, and sometimes a transfer to another House within our system. Agonising over many decisions like this can be exhausting.

While most of the time the running of the Homes is fairly regular and devoid of dramatic incidents, when these do occur they are exhausting and time consuming. A resident comes home drunk, which all the rules and precautions in the world cannot always prevent; he or she may go to bed meekly, but more likely will create a major disturbance — kicking in doors, smashing furniture or crockery, and lashing out at anyone who tries to stop them. The staff who have to cope with this can feel drained and, with good reason, frightened. Even a well-built twelve-year-old who is violent and beside himself with anger can present a real threat to an adult.

In the earlier years of running the project, drug overdosing by residents was a constant worry. With improved programmes, more staff, and greater care in the control of medication, this is now a rarity. The distribution and use of all medication is carefully controlled by staff, and it is kept under secure conditions. Nevertheless, continuing watchfulness is required, since many of our clients have used overdosing in the past as a means of gaining attention or coping with their grief.

Staff not only have to cope with stressful situations; they can also create them. As we have increasingly been able to employ experienced and mature personnel, this has occurred less and less. An employee can bring to work their own problems — a broken relationship, anger with the opposite sex because of past hurts, financial worries, and concerns about their own children. These can lead them to over-react to tense situations, growl at the residents excessively, and become confrontational rather than conciliatory with more difficult youngsters. Management are left picking up the pieces that can result from such inept handling of young people.

Experience has shown that, in an operation such as this one, the best way to mitigate undue stress is to work out and then carefully follow procedures that are clear and provide security for residents and staff. Inevitably, when this does not happen residents become confused, look for the weaknesses in the system, and exploit them. Staff supervision and the support systems that have already been described all help to alleviate the strong pressures that are inherent in youth care. We have been fortunate in not experiencing as much 'burn-out' among senior staff as some other groups in the same area of work. This is due as much to their dedication and belief in what they are doing as to the system in which they operate.

Even so, they are under great strain. There are all the broken nights, with little chance of catching up on sleep the following morning. The police knocking on one's door at 3 a.m. about a car converter, or the anxiety triggered by discovering an empty bed which means someone has taken off during the night, do not allow those in charge to sleep easily. As our numbers have grown, just getting all the staff together for a social event has become difficult. We try to get friends in to oversee the Houses when we go out for the night, but we often get called back to deal with problem behaviours.

Each time my phone rings after normal hours, I wonder what has gone wrong. It is extremely hard to go back to sleep when you have been woken to be told that a certain resident is in intensive care because of an accident or overdose. One of the worst times was when I was phoned from a camp that six of our residents were attending, to be told that two of them had drifted out to sea in a canoe, and they might drown. By this time it was getting dark. The two boys concerned had taken the boat from the camp and gone for a row without permission. Back at The Glade, we spent an anxious hour waiting for news. We used the occasion to talk to the remaining residents about obeying the rules, water safety, and how important it was not to take off on such adventures. Eventually we learnt that first one, then the other youth was safe, thanks to the skill of a man with a yacht who had seen the two drifting out to sea. Afterwards he told me that if it had been five minutes later, he could not have saved them.

For all of us who supervise youngsters in care, the responsibilities are enormous. While some parents have not been particularly successful in keeping their children out of trouble, they are quick to blame those who seemed to think they could do better. Deciding that a young person would benefit from being placed in care brings a big responsibility. Sometimes the issues are very clear, such as when a child is at risk from physical or sexual assault, or there is nowhere else for them to go. Recently a young boy who had been placed under my guardianship by the Court ran out behind a bus when returning from school, and was knocked over by a car. By the time I heard, he had been taken to hospital, and I rushed off to find out how he was. He was unconscious, and the extent of his head injuries was not yet known. As I stood beside his bed, I felt a great burden of responsibility for what had happened — not because of any neglect on my part or by the House he was living in, but because he was in my care, and I had advocated that arrangement. He turned out to be fine, and I took him away next morning, bruised and a little shocked, but not very much the worse for the accident. It was yet another reminder of how careful one has to be when assuming responsibility for other people's children.

For me, as Director of the entire operation, there is a considerable burden of administration and responsibility. For many years, my entire energies were directed toward the young residents; but more recently they have gone into staff maintenance, financial resources, public relations, and overseeing new developments. At times I yearn for the simpler days when my time was spent with the young people, and the few workers involved jelled easily as a team.

It is realistic to talk about the stresses, especially in today's more complex society, when the problems of caring for others multiply. But it would be unbalanced and untrue to give the impression that this is the full story. There is a lot of love to be found and given in caring for the young. At a recent House meeting, when the residents asked if it was because of them that several staff had recently left, tears were in my eyes as I heard their concern and felt their needs.

Frequently my phone rings with a request from someone who wants to get into social work. They usually say that they 'want to work with people, especially people with problems'. Some who come for job interviews have unrealistic expectations about working with disadvantaged youth. They are quickly disillusioned once they begin the job. Some believe that the young are eager to talk to a listening adult; they are then disappointed that it takes time and testing before most young people will share themselves with an adult, especially when they have had cause to feel let down by an older generation in the past. Others only want to sit down and counsel young people; they do not appreciate that you sometimes get closest to a young person when you are doing the dishes together or kicking a ball around.

It is almost platitudinous to state that the young learn and judge from what we do more than from what we say. They are astute and soon note our inconsistencies and our true values. Trying to impose these values on the young is futile. We need to remember that one of their developmental tasks is to sort out and test their own values.

As the years have rolled by for me, the job has become more stressful and demanding. This is not merely because of less resilience on my part; the work has become increasingly difficult, as the society in which we live has grown more violent and aggressive. Youngsters in care reflect very faithfully society's image. In this type of work one should not expect a great deal of appreciation for what one does; certainly not instant feedback. It can be delayed many years, or never be forthcoming.

The real rewards of working with the young come from enjoying the contacts of the moment and the friendships they offer, as well as the struggles, rather than the satisfactions of perceived change. Basic to such enjoyment and job satisfaction is the development and constant exercise of good listening skills. Over and beyond that, one needs good support systems to fall back on, so that energies can be renewed and objectivity maintained.

One of the things that enable people to cope with working with other people's pain is to have a life outside of the fostering or welfare work in which they are involved. Aiding the young can be so time-consuming and emotionally draining that it is easy to neglect one's own needs. To be useful to adolescents, a worker needs to maintain healthy and satisfying adult relationships. Most of those working in youth work tend to be single or separated, as the demands are very heavy on relationships. However, there are those who successfully combine the demands of the job with their own family life.

Youth work at a residential level becomes very stressful if a person tries to get their basic needs met through the work itself. If we are to avoid making children dependent, we should know why we are in the job and what we are trying to do. It can be a nice feeling to be wanted, and have people seek you out, but it is bad news for them, if they do not learn from you their own strengths and ways of self-healing and help. In youth work we have to be concerned with teaching others survival and independence skills.

Sometimes when a person has offered me their resignation, I learn for the first time that they have felt martyred or used because they have never attended to their own needs, or even made them known. In these cases a good deal of hurt is sustained and there is no chance for healing. Such staff can often feel that they are failures because a young person for whom they believed they were responsible has got into trouble again. But it is not helpful to anyone to take responsibility for another's actions. Staff meetings and supervision by a competent person help to avoid these feelings in staff working with young people. Socialising together can also help take the heat and intensity out of the demands made in constant care of the needy and neglected young. Many of the stresses Youthlink has encountered were related to being under-resourced, due to the lack of secure and consistent funding in the past. That problem has largely been addressed now. We are presently working on making our salaries competitive, so we can attract quality workers. We have moved from being a totally voluntary organisation, where everyone worked from a belief in the project, love for the young, and often a faith in me and in what I was doing, to staff in whom those motives are mixed with a valid need for financial support. A few have tended to see it only as a job, but they have been very much in the minority.

Most staff, on leaving, say that they will 'miss the kids'. They usually speak of their love for the young people and their sadness at cutting those links. They also acknowledge that they have learnt a great deal from the experience. We have a commitment to excellence, and are fired with the zeal to come as close to that as possible; so that while staff will find rewards in the work, there will most certainly be a deeply enriching and lasting benefit for the residents and all those who seek us out in crisis.

(11)
Accountability

At a time when people are becoming increasingly critical of the efficiency, relevance and cost of various treatment programmes for medical and social problems, evaluation or measurement of what is actually achieved (as opposed to what is *thought* to have been accomplished) is of special importance. Evaluation is the process of finding out whether an enterprise is operating in an optimal way.

In the 1970s, my research for my doctorate from the Auckland Medical School looked at the planning and evaluation of the residential care programme that I was then running at Lloyd Avenue, Mt Albert. What I discovered at that time, and have had confirmed since, is the great difficulty of setting up a satisfactory evaluation programme. While the literature is full of recommendations about the need for systematic planning and evaluation, practical examples of this are scarce.

I applied a system analysis model to the Home and its residents, to evaluate the programme and the changes in behaviour of residents. Seventy-two residents were involved in the study, which covered a period of fifteen months. The system was a series of parts linked together and interrelated in order to achieve a set of goals. In its planning, consideration was given to: (1) stating the objectives of the total system and measurement procedures; (2) defining the particular environment and the fixed constraints in which it operated; (3) the resources needed and used to accomplish the project within the system; (4) establishing goals; (5) the activities to meet these goals; and (6) measuring these activities.

In practical terms, as applied to the residents, the system consisted of the following components: referral of subjects; assessment of their needs, and setting long- and short-term goals to meet these; establishing the resources needed and implementing the programme, an evaluation of this, and feedback to arrange any modifications or changes necessary; follow-up and final outcome. This division could measure as well as effect change in residents' lives. The flow of information between all parts of the system was important.

This model offered two important features. First, it made possible the planning and evaluation of a remedial and developmental programme for the youth at the House. Secondly, as a model, it had wider application than the assessment of the Youthlink activities. Eventually the model was refined to look at two systems, the institution and the individual within it. The goals and activities of the individual constitute their own system; but the two systems of the community House and the individual residents are interrelated, because the effectiveness of the programme for the individual depends upon the efficiency and appropriate functioning of the House. At the same time, the extent to which the needs of individual residents are met provides an evaluation of the effectiveness of the whole system.

It is not possible in this book to go into great detail about the evaluation processes used. Only some of the most salient features can be described. These will be done under the main headings of the subsystems that constitute the system model used.

Needs: Since explicit goals are a major feature of evaluation in this approach, before goals can be established it is necessary to gauge the specific needs of the individual or the organisation concerned. Forms are used for this purpose. Individuals are referred to the Houses because it is considered that they have special needs. Through a number of steps, including initial interviews at the Crisis Centre, talks with the administrator of the House they are referred to, a visit to the House by the applicant and family or those interested in the young person's welfare, and getting to know the Special Person assigned to the resident, these needs are identified.

The completion of the structured assessment forms is the next step in the process. These cover six areas of difficulties experienced: social (making friends, sexual problems), domestic (a place to live, parental problems), occupational (holding a job, study), leisure-related (drinking problems, boredom), financial (debts, budgeting), and medical (depression or compulsions). In making these assessments, we take into account information from parents, referral agencies or others involved. The young person rates the goals in order of importance to them, and their present state is noted so that any changes can be recorded over time. In the history of the Trust, over 40 percent of needs are concerned with social and domestic issues, i.e. difficulties over interpersonal relationships.

Goals: Goals are the most crucial unit in the whole system model. These are the objectives the residents and their helpers work toward. When goals are determined, three things have to be kept in mind: that they are realistic; that they are congruent with the needs assessed; and that they allow for evaluation. The division of the goals into long-term and short-term means that the major objectives (long-term) can be achieved through a series of short steps (short-term) that make an achievement possible. For example, a girl wants to have friends; she is lonely, and has no one she can relate to. In this case, the long-term goal is to develop a friendship with one person. The purpose of this goal is to assist the girl to move away from a sense of isolation through the acquisition of a companion with whom to share experiences. Having no one person she feels close to or regards as a friend is the baseline from which any change can be measured.

The criteria are then established for measurement of the outcome. In this case, this would be that there is one person with whom the girl can feel at ease and share time, outings and experiences. A friendship will not be achieved merely by wanting one or talking about it; a number of things need to happen to reach that goal. What the goal-setting approach offers is an orderly, simple approach to a complex situation. It also means that what might in some cases seem intangible areas can be subject to more or less quantifiable measurement. As goals can be set for individuals, so they can for the institution too, for example, improved care of medication on the premises, or better behaviour at meals, or preventing theft of clothing.

Resources: The resources needed to make progress possible in the attainment of goals can vary for the institution from money to a recreation room, and for individuals from going on a weight reduction course to attending an alternative school. The variation is endless; but when the ideal resources (e.g. funding to pay full-time, top-class staff) are not within reach, then alternative resources have to be used (e.g. part-time or voluntary skilled staff).

Tasks: The attainment of any goal is a combination of factors. Breaking the goal down into logical progressive steps helps make the intent a reality. These short-term goals, when combined, make the long-term ones attainable. The number of tasks set varies according to the complexity of the goal. Gail, the girl who was working toward making a friend, for example, needed a range of resources: a dancing teacher, a hairdresser, a growth group, a psychiatrist, residents, mother and Special Person. All these were available for her, and so the tasks proceeded. In her case these included having her hair styled to improve her personal appearance, an interview with her psychiatrist to review the medication she was on and reduce her dependency on it, attending a group working on individual assertiveness, joining a dance class to attain confidence and a social skill, morning and night talks with other residents, going on outings with another resident, the development of chess skills, movement from a single to a double bedroom, a daily shower, and appropriate contact with mother (preceded by family therapy sessions).

Gail had been in the habit of visiting a very dominant mother daily, showering fortnightly, wearing ill-fitting clothing, hiding her face behind long overhanging hair, and being constantly tired due to the medication she was on, so that it was hard to get her up in the mornings. It would be wrong to think that all the enterprises for change were entered into enthusiastically by Gail. She was reluctant to take most steps, afraid and worried about change and its implications. A major breakthrough was when she got her hair restyled; suddenly she was getting affirmation about her appearance and was looking people in the eyes, rather than hiding behind her long hair. It took patience, support, successes and failures for Gail to make the slow journey toward friendship. One achievement tended to give her encouragement to move on to the next step. For these steps or tasks to continue, reviews were necessary.

Reviews: These are periods set aside to ensure that progress is being made toward both institutional and individual goals. They cover weekly, fortnightly, monthly and quarterly sessions. On some of those occasions, a check is made by resident and Special Person, for individual goals, or by Director, staff and residents, for institutional goals, to ascertain what progress is being made. These reviews ensure that goals do not get lost sight of or fail through inattention. This part of the system is closely linked with the feedback component.

Feedback: In order to make progress and for there to be change and attainment of goals, what is happening for the institution and the individual needs to be measured. This can occur through staff meetings, residents' meetings and specific surveys. Feedback should not occur only at the end or final outcome, but must be pervasive through the whole goal attainment process. An important part of feedback is that it keeps a programme or an individual on course, making sure that achievements are actually taking place. It involves affirmation, encouragement, and the incentive aspects of good or bad outcome. Attention needs to be focused on the behaviour rather than on the individual in the feedback process.

Outcome and Follow-up: This part of the system is primarily concerned with evaluation. Outcome and follow-up go together. Outcome is the review of long-term goals, both at scheduled intervals and at the termination of a programme or resident's stay. Follow-up is a later check on outcomes to determine the permanence of effects or to discover any further changes. In outcome assessment, the institutional changes are measured on a scale that covers no movement, slight improvement, some improvement, well on the way to success, very close to attainment and full attainment. The scale for individual outcomes is retrogressive movement, no real improvement, little improvement, some improvement, close to goal attainment, full goal attainment.

In my doctoral research, I found that the institutional goals were much easier to achieve than the individual ones. This is no doubt due to the fact that it is easier to change institutions than people. It is often very hard to keep young people well motivated, especially when there are many attractions pulling them in other directions, such as the apparent monetary rewards of crime, or the pressure of brothers and sisters or parents, or money in the pocket compared with the slower rewards of schooling. However, young people on the whole respond well to working for goals and the sense of achievement that working on them can bring. They like short, practical tasks that bring identifiable results. They also appreciate the feedback that comes through the evaluation process. However, some do not like written notes being kept on them, therefore confidentiality and limited access to files are important. An important benefit of using some evaluation system is that there is a defined programme, which offers security to the young. It also means that attention is given to all residents, and not only to those who are depressed or acting out or more assertive in making their needs known. Our experience has been that those most successful in our system are those who stay for more than three months in our programme.

It is easier to see how the system approach works by looking at two examples, one of an institution, the other of an individual.

Institution

The developmental goal was concerned with the Houses' relations with their surrounding communities. We wanted to foster an accepting environment in the immediate neighbourhood of The Glade and Rowan House, and also within the community generally. Three major areas were worked on over one year, as follows:

YEAR ONE

Needs: Closest neighbours to be aware of the Houses' existence and facilitate their development.

Goals: To communicate with closest neighbours on a friendly basis. This goal was broken down into:

Tasks: (a) Immediate neighbours become known to Director and administrator.

(b) Each new resident instructed on relations with neighbours and their importance. This is reviewed half-yearly.

Outcome: Through visits, all immediate neighbours became known and friendly contacts were established. A section on neighbourhood relations was added to the residents' manual. New residents were personally briefed on these when they arrived.

Attainment: For both goals, there was movement from the baseline to almost full attainment; on a scale of A to F, we reached E.

YEAR TWO

Needs: Pleasant relations with immediate neighbours, opportunities for neighbours and residents to air grievances with each other.

Goals: To open the Houses on occasion to neighbours, and provide opportunities for discussion of difficulties.

Tasks: (a) An Open House for immediate neighbours once a year.

(b) An open discussion on each occasion. Reviewed annually.

Outcome: Morning tea at The Glade had 62 percent attendance, afternoon tea at Rowan House 75 percent attendance.

Attainment: Task (a) got a D scoring — well on the way to success. Task (b) scored F – full success.

YEAR THREE

Needs: Community to be aware of Houses and their functions.

Goals: To monitor publicity about the Houses in the community, and to have community involvement.

Tasks: (a) All publicity screened by the Director.

(b) Director and others to visit anyone in the neighbourhood affected adversely by residents' actions.

(c) A half-yearly project to benefit people in the neighbourhood to be undertaken by residents and staff. Reviewed annually.

Outcome and attainment: All publicity was screened — F, full success; five visits were made to homes — F; and projects were completed on four occasions — F.

Individual

Phillip was the second in a family of five children, living in the South Island. His father was a plumber, his mother cared for the children at home. The home was small, adding to family stress.

Phillip was referred to us when he was fifteen because of constant stealing, going back to when he was eight, and non-conforming behaviour at home: refusing to do what his mother asked, talking back to her, picking on the younger children — including a sister who was blind — and antagonising everyone. He never appeared to show any remorse for his actions. The family had tried to cover up his thieving, but could not do so when he used a friend's bank book to steal and bought a bicycle with the money.

At the initial interview, it was stated the Phillip had been hyperactive as a child. It had been thought that he might have a hearing difficulty, but after tests it was established that he simply blocked out everything he didn't want to hear. It was also mentioned that Phillip found schooling difficult, not through lack of intelligence but because of his inability to concentrate.

A family interview took place and it was decided that Phillip should move to The Glade. On moving in, Phillip stated his problems and needs and, with us, set goals for himself to achieve during his period with Youthlink. During one of his goal-setting sessions, the youth recalled with shame, and some anger, being caught stealing something in the classroom the previous year. He was stood in front of the class, who were invited by the teacher to call him a thief, which they did in unison. One of the problem areas he noted was a severe difficulty in making friends or getting on with his peers.

While Phillip presented a somewhat arrogant attitude, behind the façade was a young man wanting a lot of recognition and reassurance. He masked his feelings, and pretended he 'didn't care'. He also often showed a lack of compassion for others, and readily picked on others' weaknesses in a hurtful way. It became clear that he had been into much more stealing than had ever been uncovered previously. Phillip showed a low sense of self-respect, often belittling himself. He also grieved over his poor relationship with his father, whom he believed paid little attention to him. He had stolen from the home as well as from his father, and felt his father would never forgive him or trust him again, so he believed there was no point in trying further. As a result, he had used destructive means of gaining attention.

The *needs* he listed were: social — to make friends, learn to relate to the opposite sex, improve his personal appearance (get rid of acne); domestic — work through his problems with his parents, especially his father; occupational — overcome his study difficulties, get a secure job he will be able to hold; leisure — learn to budget his money; medical — overcome his anxiety and tension, overcome feelings of depression.

The *goals* set were both long- and short-term. The long-term ones were to return home, to complete his sixth form schooling, to reach the Almorah level in the House and remain there, and to overcome his stealing habits. The short-term goals to those ends were to establish a close friendship with one other person, preferably a resident of The Glade; build his self-confidence, through watching his diet (acne problem), improving personal hygiene (daily shower, change of clothes and washing his face morning and night); regular contact with his family through phone calls, letters and holiday visits; apologise to residents when he put them down; confide in his Special Person when he felt tempted to steal, or if he had stolen something, to admit this to his confidant; get a part-time job, in order to improve his wardrobe; take an active part in sports, exercising daily in the gym at The Glade; use the weekday homework period to get help through the teacher present, to improve his reading skills; save part of his weekly pocket money for future needs; and take part in family therapy sessions.

Mistakes were made by Phillip in the course of his stay. Against our advice, he attended a highly competitive school, which he soon dropped out of, and then became depressed over his sense of failure. He settled in better to the Glade School, and made reasonable progress. He gave up truanting, which had been part of his earlier behaviour. He often stole while with us, at least in the first few months; these thefts were mostly of small items, such as socks, knives, forks and keys. Gradually this magpie approach to taking things disappeared. Phillip did have to face consequences for his behaviour, such as having to face up to shopkeepers and others from whom he stole, or paying back money owed from his job earnings.

On a number of occasions our therapist and family therapist went with Phillip to his home for work with family relations. The youth's hopes were always raised by such meetings, and he would argue that now he was ready to return home. But the family and he were not ready, and tearfully he would return to The Glade. The father at these sessions often stated that he felt what the boy needed was more punishment, as he had always got off too lightly following his thefts. He was keen on a 'short sharp shock' treatment, perhaps in a youth reform prison.

One of the sad things for Phillip to cope with was the comment from both parents that since he had moved out, life was much pleasanter in the house. Other things emerged in the course of the family sessions: Phillip's mother felt neglected by her husband, they had no sex life, and he was more interested in the birds he kept than in her or the children. In fact, the whole unsatisfactory nature of the parents' relationship emerged, so they had to work on that area before Phillip would ever be able to return home.

By the time he left The Glade, many of the tasks or short-term goals were achieved. He did return home, though by the time he did so, the father had left it, as the barrenness of the marriage relationship had became obvious. He completed his secondary schooling, though he did not pass in all subjects in the state examinations. This was close to attainment of that goal. He attained full success in terms of remaining an Almorah, at least for the last two months of his stay.

The goal of overcoming his stealing habits was less successful. He was stealing less frequently when he left, and the items were of smaller value; however, he seemed unable to break the habit completely. We felt that he had been unable to establish himself in his father's eyes the way he wanted, and this affected his stealing pattern. Often, after a setback with his father, we would notice an increase in stealing.

We followed up on Phillip some months after he left The Glade. He seemed to have assumed a more responsible role in the home, though he had difficulty coping with his mother's relationship with another man. At one stage he had taken off from home and come back to us for a few days, while he sorted his difficulties out. He seemed to progress after that point, though he has occasionally phoned his former therapist for support.

As the reader could imagine, the recording of all the data on this and other residents fills many pages. It is a record of progress and failure, as well as of interventions to change behaviour. It is essential for evaluation that records are kept and progress is regularly monitored. The initial measurement as to where a person is at, compared with the time they leave Youthlink, is basic to estimating goal attainment.

Planning in this way also provides a sense of direction for all those involved in arranging or monitoring programmes for young people, since objectives are defined and procedures are clear. Problems arise when staff are not committed to the processes, or to meeting the requirements of form-filling. The system approach offers a methodical step-by-step movement through a planned programme, rather than a trial-and-error or guess work approach.

In general, the system approach appeared to be simple to apply, and of general applicability. It allowed a mixing of different needs and groups, and provided opportunities for working out interpersonal differences. Finally, since the goal–setting processes were concerned not so much with symptoms but with improved personal functioning, undue attention to whatever psychodynamics were operative was avoided.

Conclusion

The story of Youthlink is the story of thousands of young people, their families, and those who have worked in and supported the project over sixteen years. The distance we have come has been the fruit of their energies, contribution, or sometimes lack of it; but we have tried to learn from our apparent failures, so these too have contributed to the growth of Youthlink.

At times I become worried at the responsibility I personally carry, and the size and scope of the whole organisation. But I find reassurance in the quality of the people who work with me, and support the project. I am also concerned that given my prominence, the credit for what is done may be directed toward me, whereas it belongs to the whole dedicated group who work to improve the quality of life for deprived youngsters.

In a sense I am an optimist, as I am always hoping that the latest tuning or radical change (such as a new administrator or staff member) will make the whole thing work smoothly and efficiently. The reality is usually different, and something else goes amiss. I remind myself that I am mostly dealing with young people, and they bring all sorts of complexities to the work. But it is hard not to get disappointed when things go wrong, and someone steals a car, fights with another resident, smashes up our furniture or leadlights, runs away, steals from us, sells their new clothes, or offends a neighbour. We go through all the self-examinations and seeking of accountability for these events, and we make residents face the consequences; but it is hard to cope with when lots of caring and weeks of effort seem to have had little effect on a given person.

There are the really poignant moments, such as the farewells to residents, when they speak from their heart, often briefly, but honestly, about their feelings at leaving. Those are good moments in our history. It is also moving when they talk about their hurts — their mother just having been beaten up by their father, or the trip home for the holidays that was so eagerly anticipated, but ended in failure after only one or two days. The tears flow readily, though some tend to take the hurt into themselves. In such moments of sharing, the façades or toughness and untouchableness fade, and the very vulnerable and malleable young person can be seen.

Overall, most residents eventually show warmth of response

and openness once trust is established. This helps us all keep pumping energy into them and the project. There are developments in residents that reassure us and provide the will to keep on trying. One of the rewarding experiences for me came last year, when I was presenting a talk on adolescent needs to a refresher course seminar for Auckland secondary school teachers. As part of my presentation I involved, near the end of the session, two residents who had been with us several years. I talked with them about their problems, why they had got into trouble and what they were presently doing. The audience of teachers asked them many questions.

The one that remains in my memory was responded to by sixteen-year-old Michael. A teacher had asked him a number of personal questions, and concluded by asking, 'Who would you most like to be like, when you grow up?' I know Michael fairly well, and felt his response was a genuine one. He said, 'Like Felix'. It was humbling, yet gratifying, because Michael had learnt that I cared. That kind of learning makes it all worthwhile.